Famous Aircraft
in
ORIGAMI
18 Realistic Models

José María Chaquet Ulldemolins

DOVER PUBLICATIONS, INC.
Mineola, New York

To Beatriz,
for her support and inspiration

Bibliographical Note

This Dover edition, first published in 2008, is a new English translation of
Aviones de Colección: Modelos Realistas en Papiroflexia, originally published
in Spanish by Editorial Miguel A. Salvatella, S. A., Barcelona, Spain, 2005,
and includes all of the original diagrams, illustrations, and photos. The photos are originally by Juan Alberto Martínez García. This Dover edition is published by special arrangement with Editorial Miguel A. Salvatella, S.A., Calle
Santo Domingo 5, 08012 Barcelona, Spain.

Library of Congress Cataloging-in-Publication Data

Chaquet Ulldemolins, José María.
    [Aviones de colección. English]
    Famous aircraft in origami : 18 realistic models / José María Chaquet
Ulldemolins.
        p. cm.
    ISBN-13: 978-0-486-46592-0
    ISBN-10: 0-486-46592-6
    1. Paper airplanes. 2. Origami. I. Title.

TL778.C4413 2008
736'.982—dc22

                                                                    2007046752

Manufactured in the United States of America
Dover Publications, Inc., 31 East 2nd Street, Mineola, N.Y. 11501

Contents

1. Contents 5

2. List of Models 6

3. Prologue – by Fernando Gilgado 8

4. Introduction 9

5. Symbols 11

6. Folding Instructions 12

    Airbus A320 12

    F-117 Night Hawk 17

    Space Shuttle 20

    Bell Model 209 Huey Cobra 23

    Messerschmitt Bf 109K 25

    Engineless Glider 29

    Supermarine Spitfire 32

    Panavia Tornado 37

    F-18 Hornet 42

    Schweizer-Hughes 300 45

    Autogyro Cierva C.30 48

    Autogyro Cierva C.19 51

    Eurofighter Typhoon 54

    McDonnell Douglas MD-80 59

    C-212 Aviocar 64

    Bell/Boeing V-22 Osprey 69

    Fokker Dr. I, The Red Baron 74

    Sopwith F.1 Camel 79

7. Techniques, Insignias, and Finishing Touches 87

8. Photographs 91

List of Models

Airbus A320
Page 12

F-117 Night Hawk
Page 17

Space Shuttle
Page 20

Bell Model 209 Huey Cobra
Page 23

Messerschmitt Bf 109K
Page 25

Engineless Glider
Page 29

Supermarine Spitfire
Page 32

Panavia Tornado
Page 37

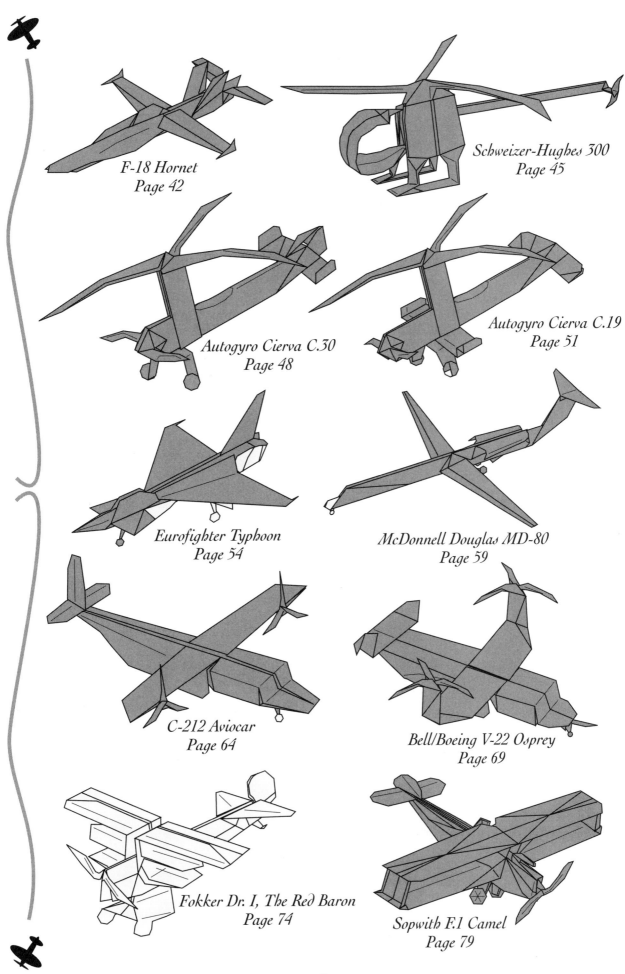

F-18 Hornet
Page 42

Schweizer-Hughes 300
Page 45

Autogyro Cierva C.30
Page 48

Autogyro Cierva C.19
Page 51

Eurofighter Typhoon
Page 54

McDonnell Douglas MD-80
Page 59

C-212 Aviocar
Page 64

Bell/Boeing V-22 Osprey
Page 69

Fokker Dr. I, The Red Baron
Page 74

Sopwith F.1 Camel
Page 79

Prologue
by Fernando Gilgado

Origami is the art of folding paper. Although it originated in Japan, through the years it has become a hobby shared by many people around the world and even part of popular culture in many countries. I am sure everyone remembers having folded paper airplanes at school. Maybe its success is based on the values concealed behind each fold in the paper. Not only is it a fun and inexpensive hobby, it also has great educational value, since it helps develop spatial intelligence, teaches concepts in geometry, and improves dexterity.

Since origami is such a widespread activity, there are many books on the subject. Among them, there are several on paper airplanes; the airplanes fly well, but are far from being faithful reproductions of the original airplanes. There are not many books focused on reproducing detailed, realistic models. This book presents paper airplanes that do not fly; instead, their merit lies in their faithful design. Once again, we are proving that, in origami, we can fold any figure without resorting to using scissors or glue.

When it comes time to design the figures, it is important to be really motivated, since it is a difficult and complex task that requires an investment of many hours of work.

For this reason, creators usually choose subject matters they really like.

We often find that folders who are passionate about math, for example, love designing geometrical figures. Others may like monsters and choose to create all kinds of fantastic beings.

Other people are interested in insects and relentlessly design all kinds of bugs.

In José María's case, we have a young engineer who loves aviation. He is part of the new generation of Spanish origami aficionados, whose skills equal those of the great international masters. His models show his passion for flying machines, their history, and aerodynamic shapes, encompassing the knowledge passed on by generations of experienced engineers. Ever since he became known to the world of origami, he has stood out because of his constant evolution. He has surprised us with increasingly complex and detailed models, and is always willing to share his interest in airplanes. The book that you have in your hands is the fruit of his labors.

Therefore, I hope you enjoy the models found here and, fold after fold, you can reminisce about the fascinating history of aviation. Above all, I hope you discover the magic of origami.

Introduction

Dear reader and origami aficionado: I am pleased to introduce my first book, called "Famous Aircraft in Origami," [an English translation of "Aviones de Colección"]. In it, I have tried to combine two of my greatest passions: aeronautics and origami.

I have been enjoying the art of origami for many years now. During this time, I have seen only a few origami books with realistic-looking airplane models. There are many wonderful flying airplanes, and more complex ones that cannot fly, but they do not depict any real airplane in particular. This is how I got the idea to write this book.

Eighteen models are included, all of them reproductions of actual airplanes (or helicopters, autogyros, etc.) I tried to choose those that played important roles in aviation history, or those I thought might be interesting to fold. With regard to Spanish aviation history, we have to highlight the autogyros designed by engineer Juan de la Cierva. There are also a couple pairs of classic airplanes flown during the two World Wars: the Fokker Dr. I and the Sopwith F.1 Camel from World War I, and the Messerschmitt Bf 109K and the Supermarine Spitfire from World War II.

There are many trends in the origami world. I am a conservative kind of guy, so I do not use cuts and prefer to start with a square piece of paper. All of the models shown in this book follow this principle,

except the Airbus A320, which uses two rectangular sheets of paper.

I wanted to add this airplane to the collection because it is easy to fold and the finished product is impressive.

Regarding the folding methods: I have tried to include models that are not too complex. Most can be folded in fewer than 50 steps. I have not used the Tree Theory for making the bases; or at least not directly. As you can see in the folding instructions for each figure, most use traditional bases or variations of these: the fish, bird, frog, blintz frog, etc. Thus, the initial steps for all of the models are simple to follow and recognizable by experienced origami enthusiasts.

The models are presented in increasing order of difficulty. Along with each model, we have included some information about the real airplane. Crease patterns are also shown, so that you can better understand how the paper fits together in the folded model. Three different views of the folded model are also shown, which are very useful for the final steps. The number seen in one of the views is the "reduction factor." This is the ratio between the folded model and the paper's initial length. Therefore, if a model has a reduction factor of 0.6, and we started with a square whose sides were 7.8 inches (20 cm) long, we would end up with a figure that was 7.8 x 0.6 = 4.7 inches (12 cm) long.

All diagrams use the standard international symbols. This way, as with sheet music, anyone in any country can understand the folding instructions.

Nevertheless, some complex steps include a short explanation to help the reader.

The "Techniques, Insignias, and Finishing Touches" section, includes recommendations on what paper to use, as well as descriptions of certain techniques that will make the models look more realistic.

I will not keep you any longer. The only thing left is to do is invite you to fold one of the airplanes. I hope you enjoy this book!

José María

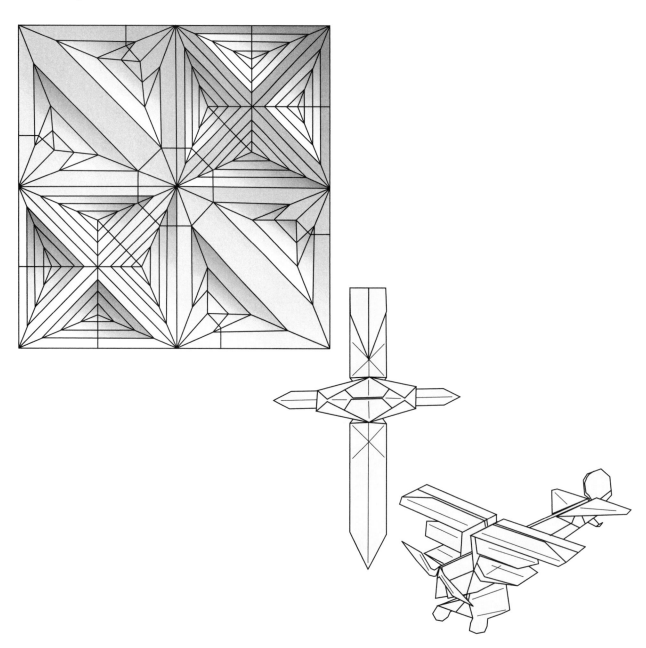

Symbols

—————— Edge of the paper

—————— Mark from a previous fold

– – – – – Valley fold

–··–··–·· Mountain fold

················ X-ray (hidden) fold

Fold direction

Fold back

Unfold and pull the paper out

Turn the model over

Enlarged view

Reduced view

Sink

Equal distances

Equal angles

Right angle

180° Rotate to the indicated degree in the direction of the arrow

Start with the dark side facing down

Start with the dark side facing up

Use a sheet of paper with the same color on both sides

Repeat as many times as the number of marks in the arrow

2-5 Repeat indicated steps

Look at the model from this perspective

Airbus A320

*T*he A320's first flight was in February of 1987. Aviation companies from Germany, France, Great Britain, Spain, and Belgium participated in the project. It was the first passenger aircraft with a "fly-by-wire" control system and advanced avionics in the cabin. It can transport up to 170 passengers at a time. A variation of the A320 is the A319, which has a smaller fuselage (110.9 feet / 33.8 meters) and capacity for 142 passengers. Another version, the A321, has an extended fuselage (146 feet / 44.5 meters) and can accommodate up to 220 people. This is the only model that does not start with the traditional square piece of paper. You will need two rectangles: one 4 x 1 piece for the fuselage and one 2 x 1 piece for the wings.

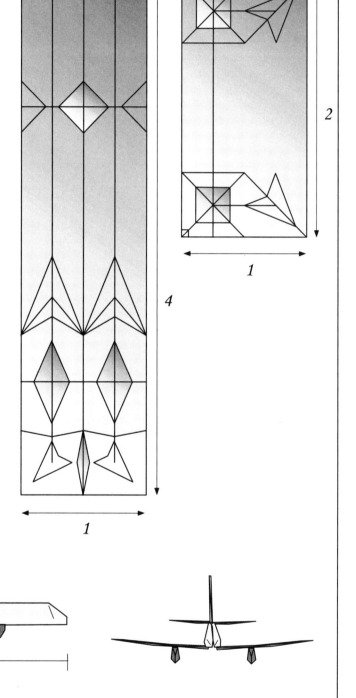

Folding of the fuselage

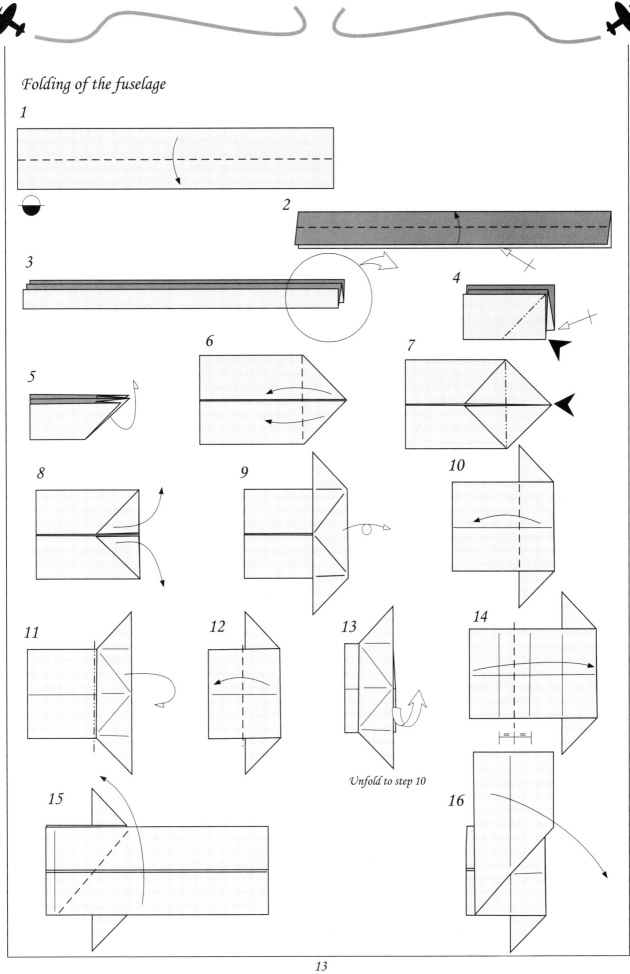

1

2

3

4

5

6

7

8

9

10

11

12

13

Unfold to step 10

14

15

16

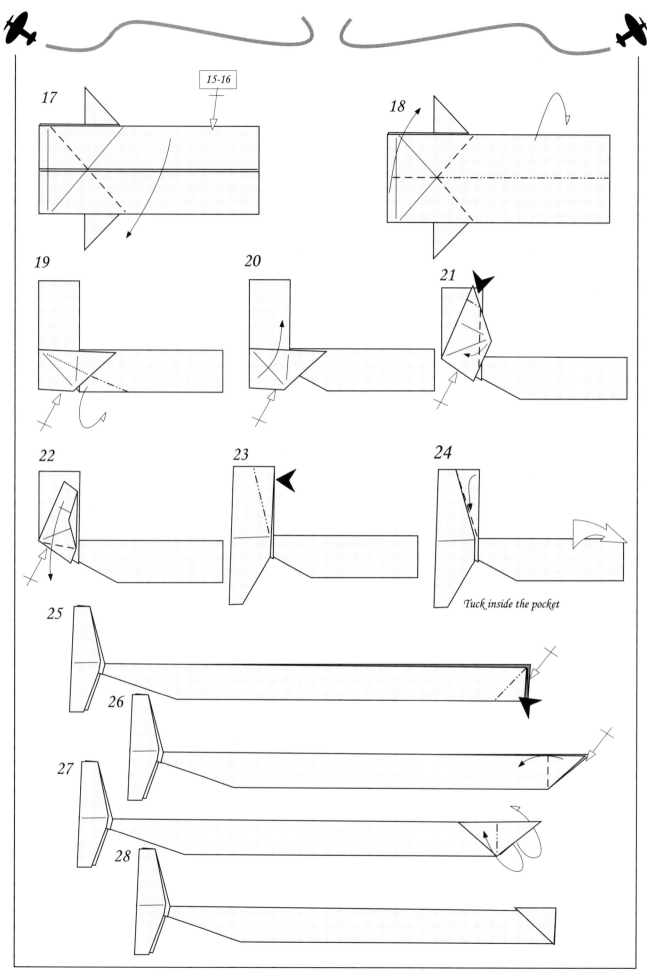

17

15-16

18

19

20

21

22

23

24

Tuck inside the pocket

25

26

27

28

Folding of the wing

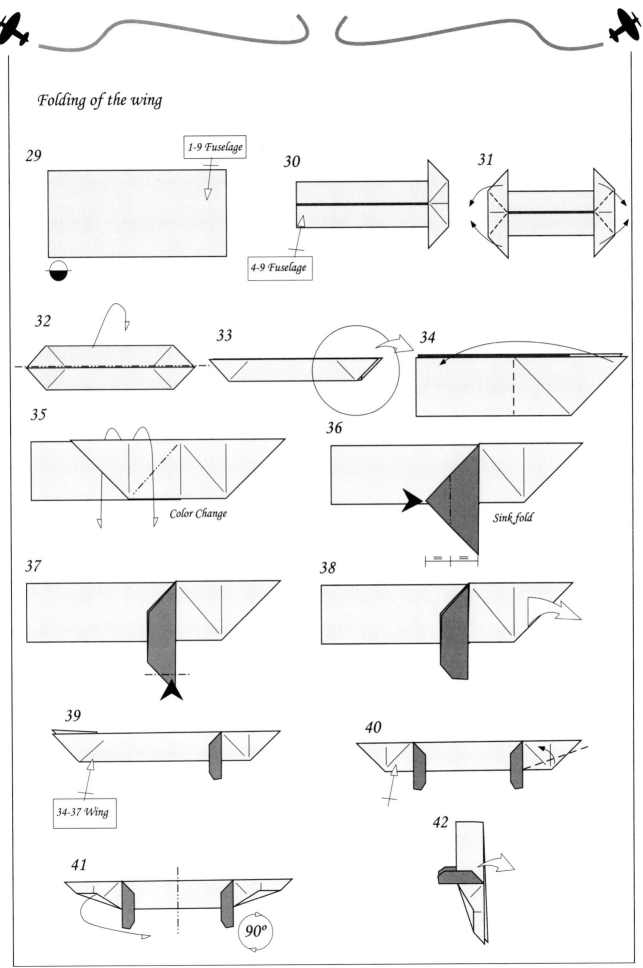

29

1-9 Fuselage

4-9 Fuselage

30

31

32

33

34

35

Color Change

36

Sink fold

37

38

39

34-37 Wing

40

41

90°

42

Interlocking of the fuselage and the wing

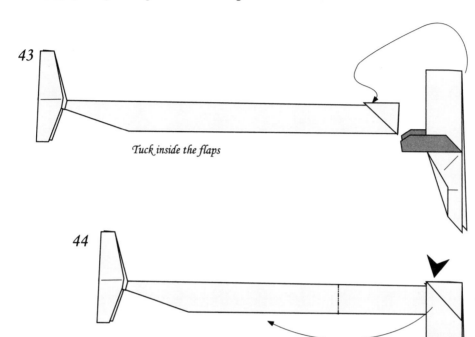

43

Tuck inside the flaps

44

45

Fold the nose asymmetrically in order to close it

46

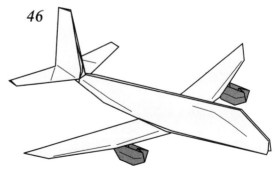

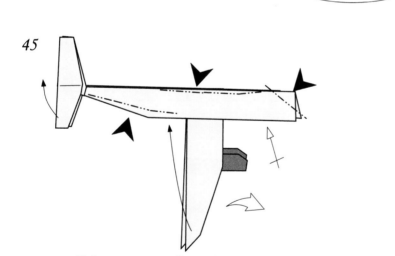

F-117
Night Hawk

*T*he F-117 has an unmistakable silhouette, recognizable from any angle. Its polyhedral shape reflects radar signals in all directions, making it virtually invisible, including to AWACS. To reduce costs and maintain secrecy, whenever possible, components and equipment from other currently in-service airplanes were used. The configuration of the wing in this airplane requires digital flight control. The quadruple-redundant F-16 GEC system was chosen. The exhaust nozzles have narrow openings and vertical fins that help to transfer heat. These openings are surrounded by a heat-resistant ceramic material, similar to that used on the Space Shuttle.

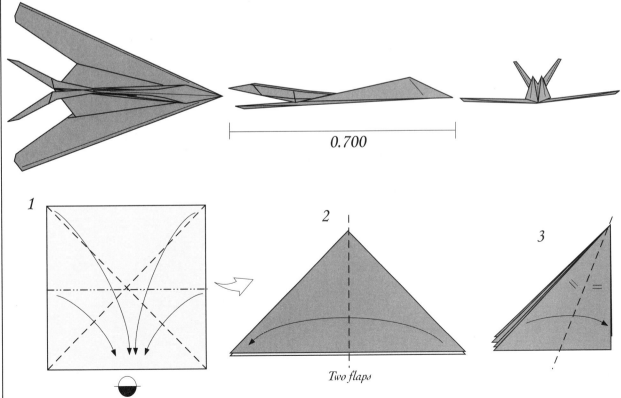

0.700

1

2

Two flaps

3

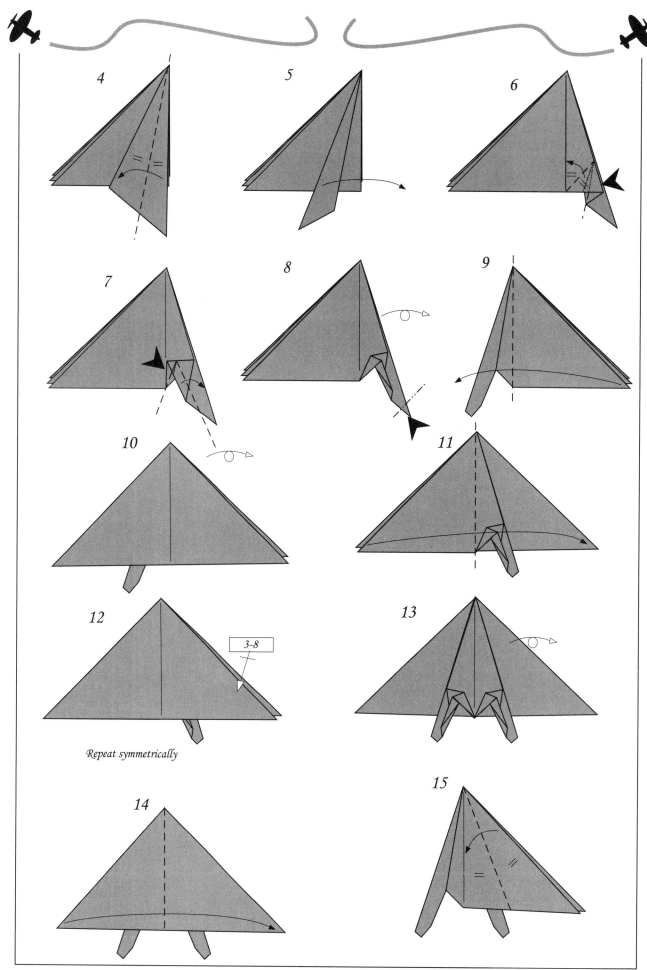

4

5

6

7

8

9

10

11

12

3-8

Repeat symmetrically

13

14

15

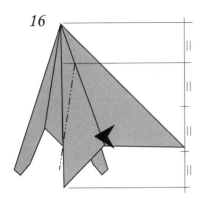

16

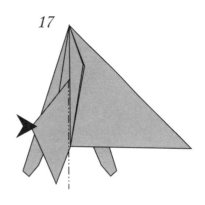

17

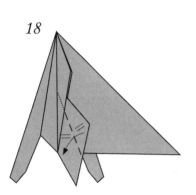

18

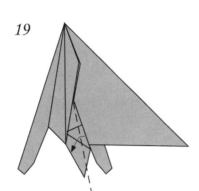

19

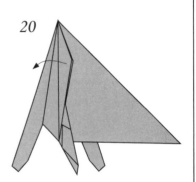

20

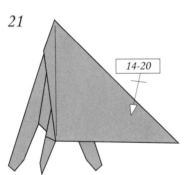

21

14-20

Repeat symmetrically

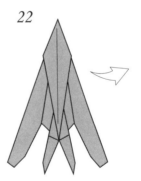

22

Perform a V-shape on the tails and
a 3D-shape on the cockpit

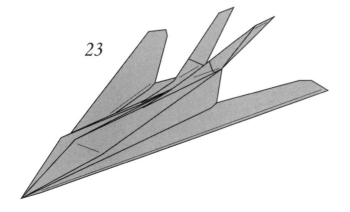

23

Space Shuttle

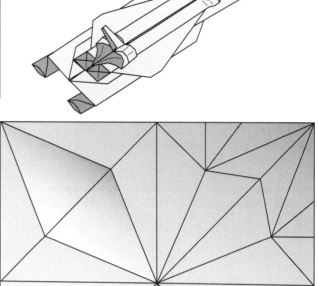

The Space Shuttle has been key to the development of the United States' space program. the Shuttle's main advantage is that it is reusable. It is propelled by several rocket engines, which detach when it reaches a certain altitude. After completing its mission, the shuttle must "reenter" the atmosphere, a very delicate maneuver due to the high temperatures that are reached. It then lands like a glider. Four units were built. Two of them were lost: the Columbia and the Challenger. Discovery and Atlantis remain in service. These machines, along with the Russian-engineered crafts, allowed for the construction, and are needed to resupply the International Space Station.

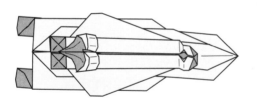

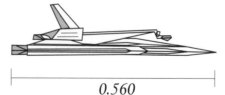

0.560

1

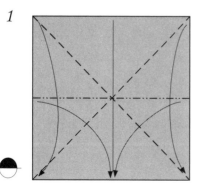

2

Double open sink fold

3

4

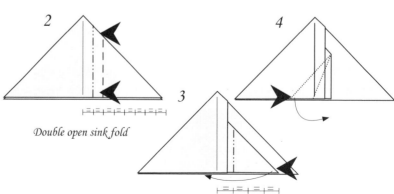

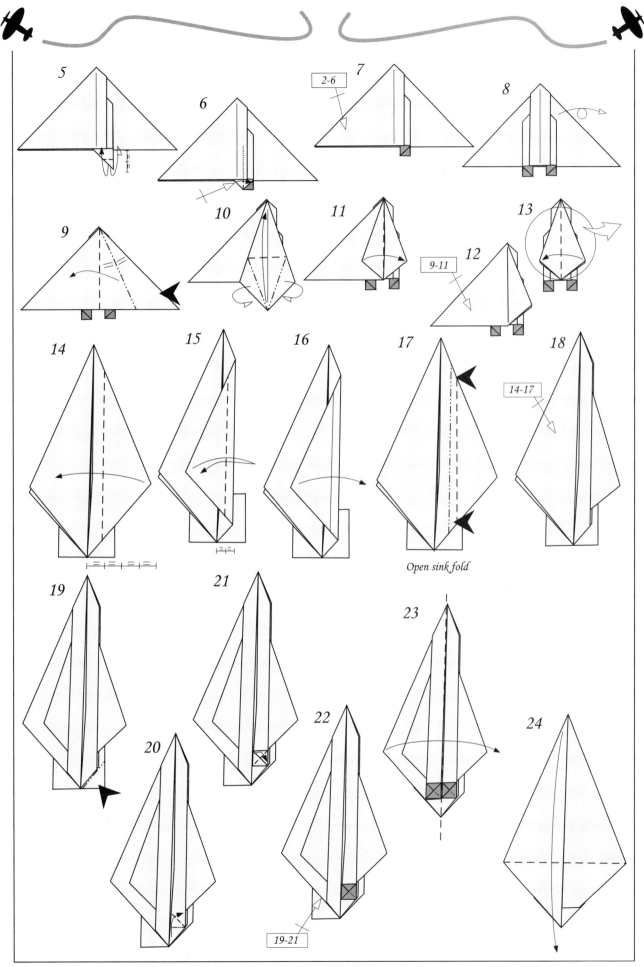

5

6

7 2-6

8

9

10

11

12 9-11

13

14

15

16

17

Open sink fold

18 14-17

19

20

21

22

23

24

19-21

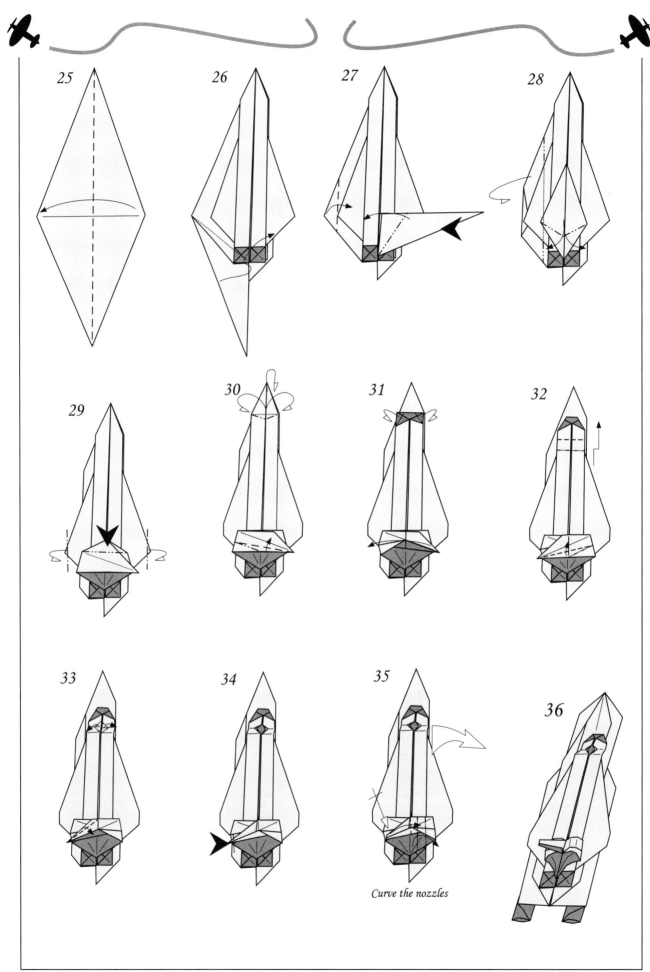

25

26

27

28

29

30

31

32

33

34

35

Curve the nozzles

36

Bell Model 209
Huey Cobra

*C*reated in 1965 as a private project, the Huey Cobra was designed to fulfill an urgent need for a provisional armed helicopter, while waiting for another project—which was never completed—to enter service. After the Vietnam War, the Cobra was improved with TOW missiles. A Lycoming turboshaft (1800 shp) drives the composite rotor. The modernized cabin is compatible with night vision goggles, pilot HUD and new guided weapons systems, as well as integrated navigation and communication equipment. The seats and cabin are armored to protect them from small-arms fire.

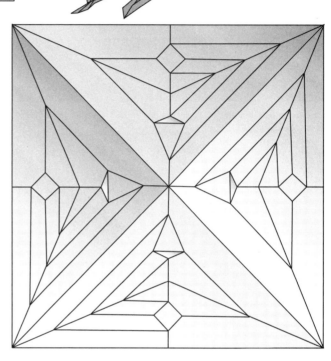

0.561

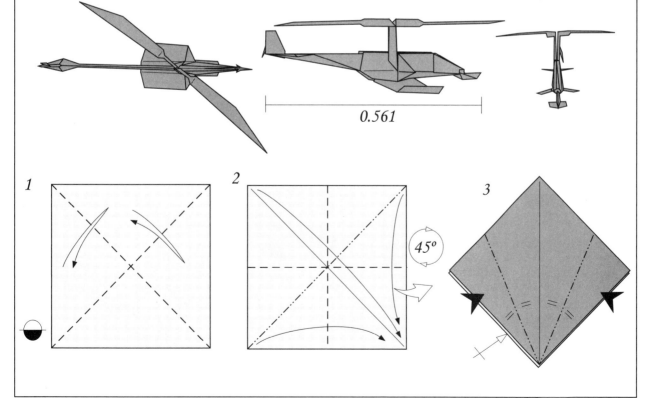

1

2

45°

3

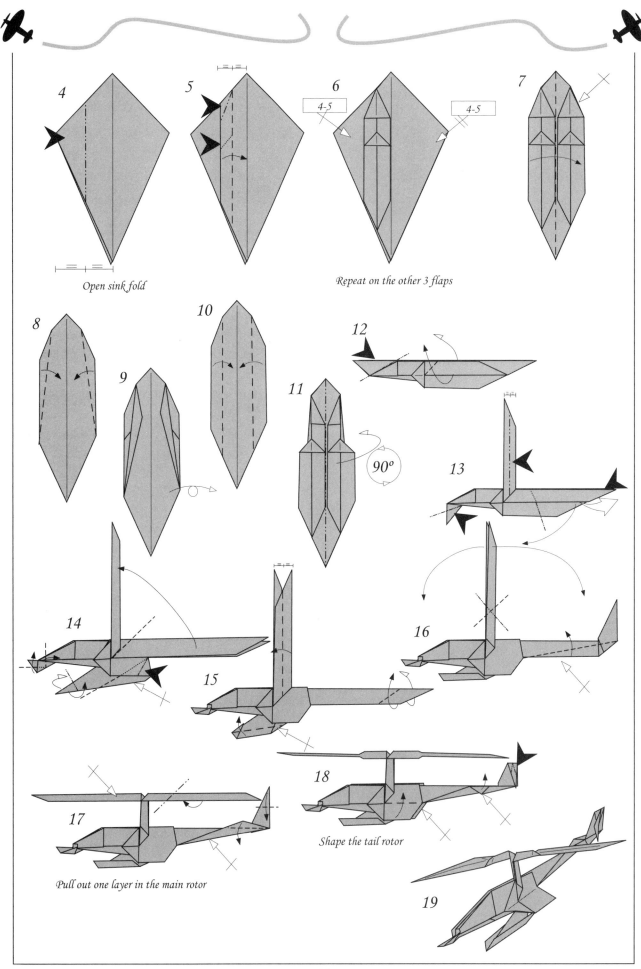

4

5

6 4-5 4-5

7

Open sink fold

Repeat on the other 3 flaps

8

10

12

9

11 **90°**

13

14

15

16

17 18

Pull out one layer in the main rotor

Shape the tail rotor

19

Messerschmitt Bf 109K

This famous World War II German airplane is the eternal rival of the also famous British Spitfire fighter plane. Many versions were made. The Bf 109K was one of the last ones made. The first model left the assembly line in August of 1944. It came with a 1.2 inch (30mm) cannon and two 0.5 inch (13mm) machine guns above the engine, standard. It had a V-12 Daimler-Benz engine with liquid cooling that drove a three-blade propeller (9.8 feet / 3 meters, in diameter). The fuel tank was located behind the pilot and had a capacity of 105 gallons (400 liters). To improve its autonomy, some airplanes had an 881 pound (300-kg) launchable fuel tank mounted under the fuselage.

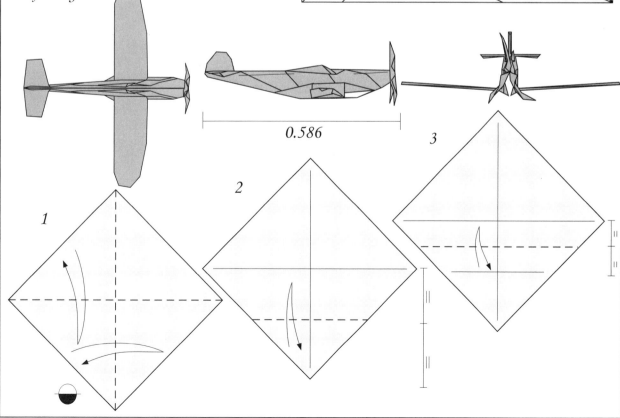

0.586

1

2

3

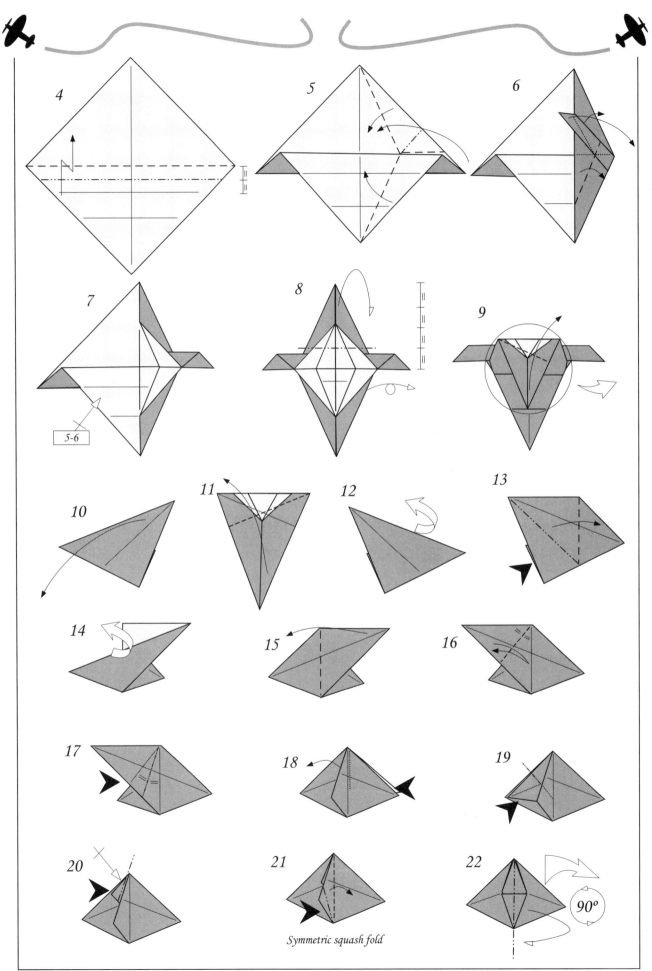

Symmetric squash fold

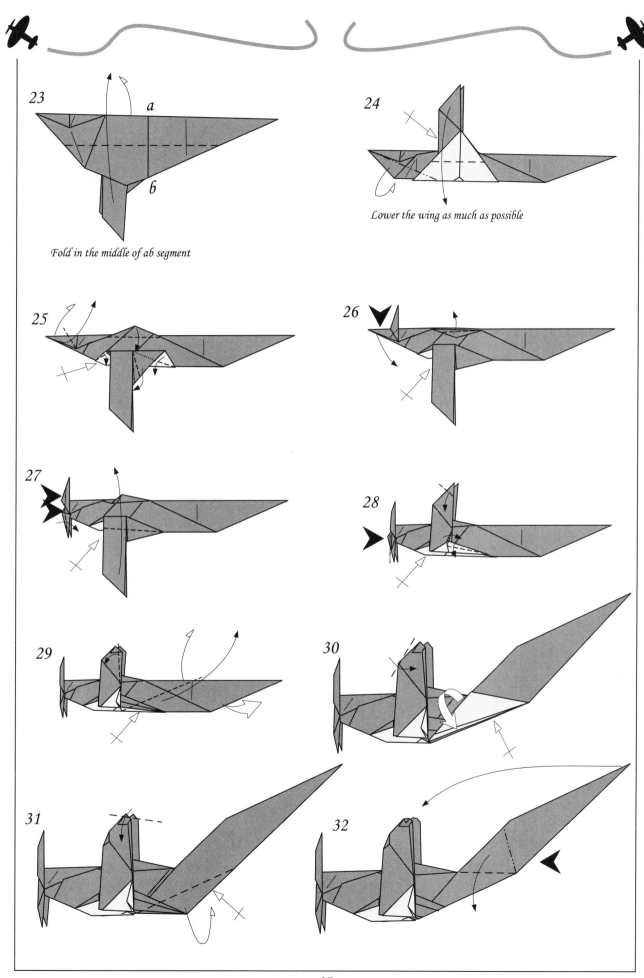

23

a

6

Fold in the middle of ab segment

24

Lower the wing as much as possible

25

26

27

28

29

30

31

32

33

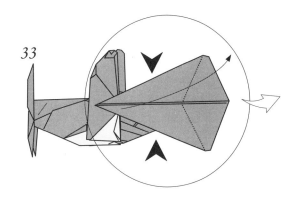

34

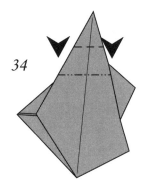

Double sink fold

35

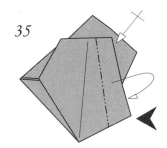

36

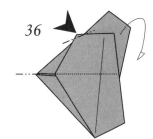

37

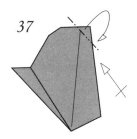

38

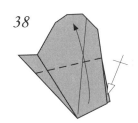

39

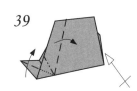

40

41

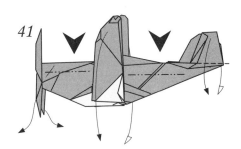

Pull down the wings and the tail.
Curve the fuselage.

42

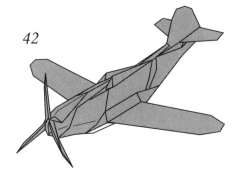

Engineless Glider

One of the most authentic modes of flight is engineless flight. These are small and very lightweight gliders, with one or two seats, and a meticulous aerodynamic design. To take off, it needs to be towed by a powered airplane. When a certain height is reached, they perform the "release." The main features of these airplanes are their very high glide ratios and their ability to stay airborne for long periods of time, thanks to pockets of warm air called "thermals." Air brakes are used when landing to reduce the glide ratio. To make transporting the airplane easier, a great majority of these planes allow for removal of the wings.

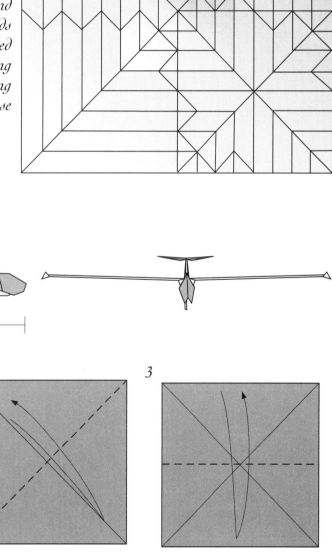

0.425

1

2

3

Cockpit color upside

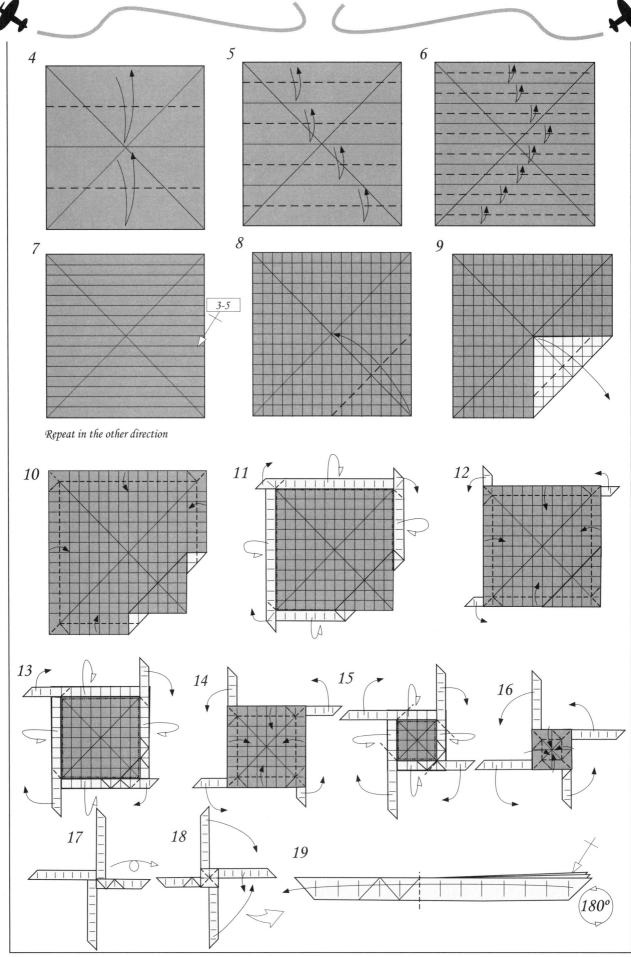

4

5

6

7

3-5

Repeat in the other direction

8

9

10

11

12

13

14

15

16

17

18

19

180°

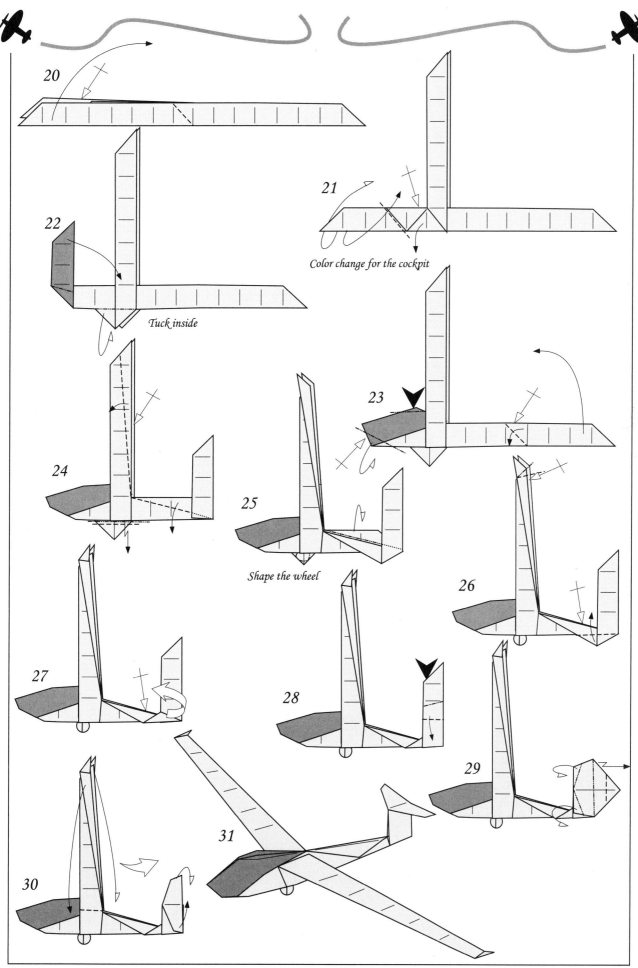

20

21

Color change for the cockpit

22

Tuck inside

23

24

25

Shape the wheel

26

27

28

29

30

31

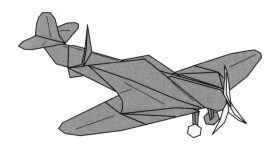

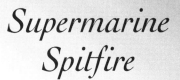

Supermarine Spitfire

*D*uring most of World War II, the Spitfire and the Bf 109K saw a lot of action. A pilot's abilities were crucial. Elliptical wings gave this famous British fighter plane an unmistakable appearance. Many versions were made. The first ones had a V-12 Rolls-Royce Merlin engine. The constant-speed three-blade propeller was more than 9.8 feet (3 meters) in diameter. The Mk VC version was modified to operate in the sands of the Libyan desert and in other hot climates. These machines stood out because of the large sand filters located below the nose. One of the last versions, known as the Griffon, were so good that they stayed in service until the beginning of the jet-engine era.

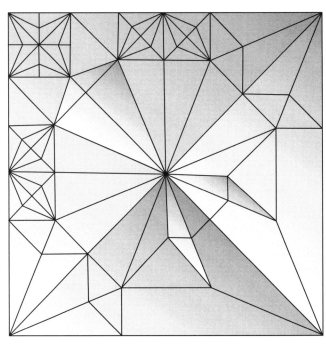

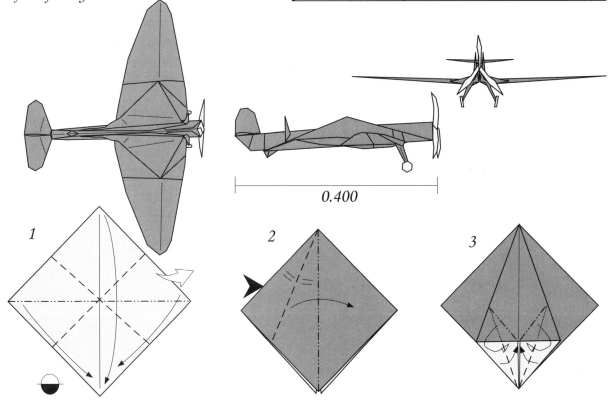

0.400

1

2

3

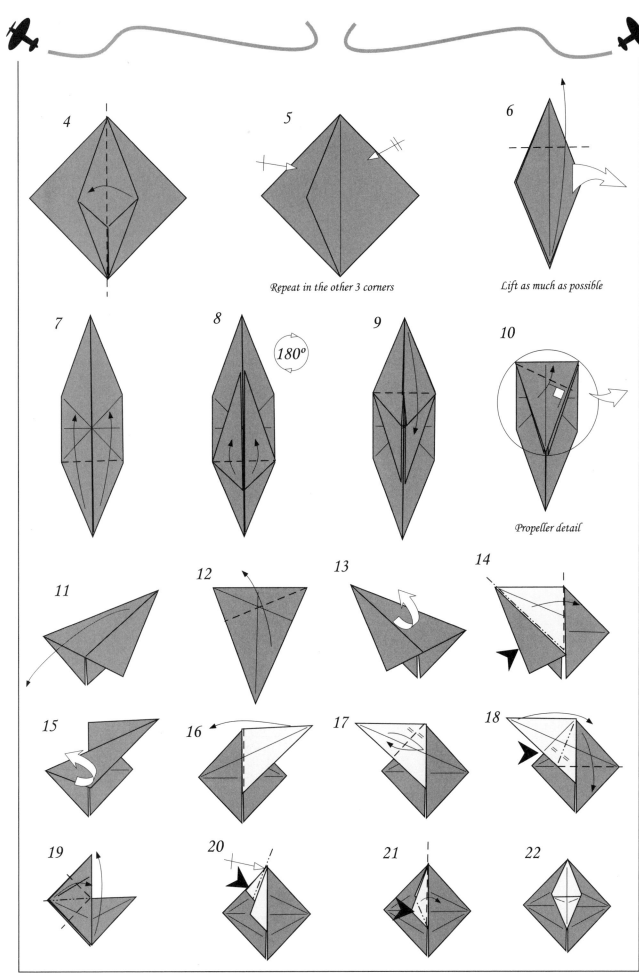

4

5

Repeat in the other 3 corners

6

Lift as much as possible

7

8

180°

9

10

Propeller detail

11

12

13

14

15

16

17

18

19

20

21

22

23

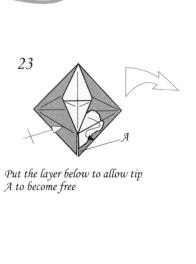

*Put the layer below to allow tip
A to become free*

24

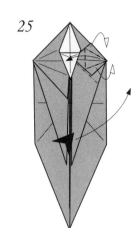

25

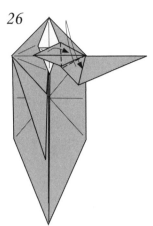

26

27

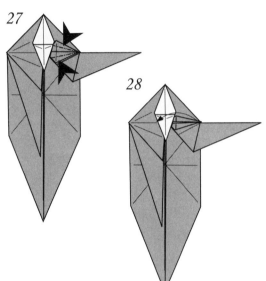

28

29

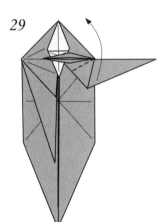

*Open using the fold done
in step 26*

30

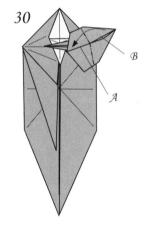

B

A

*Now the model is not flat.
Fold with line A coinciding
with line B.*

31

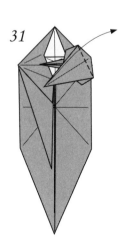

32

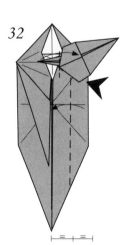

33

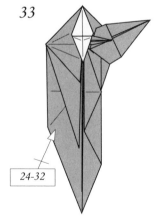

24-32

34

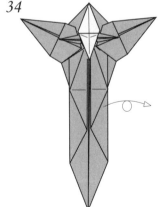

Repeat on the other side

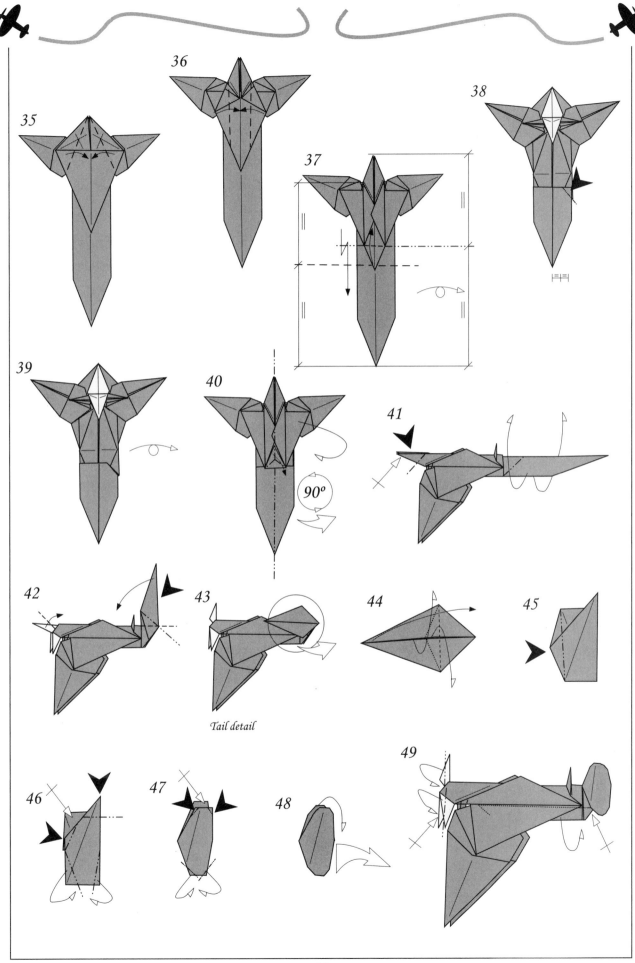

35

36

37

38

39

40

41

42

43

44

45

Tail detail

46

47

48

49

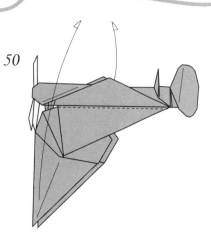

50

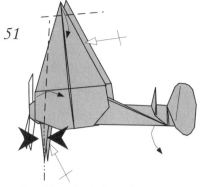

51

Pull out the tail wheel at side
of the fold done in step 38

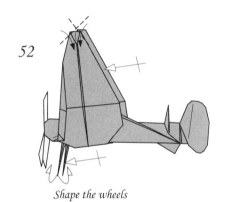

52

Shape the wheels

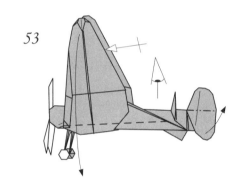

53

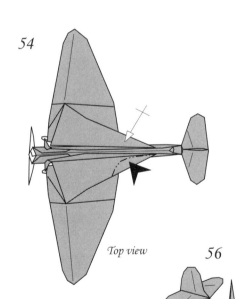

54

Top view

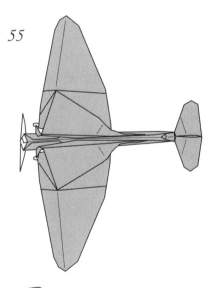

55

56

Panavia Tornado

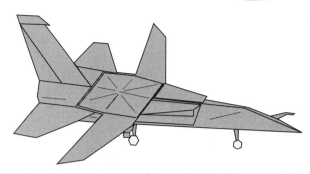

*T*he tornado, a European combat airplane, was made by Great Britain, Germany, and Italy. It has modest dimensions and is powered by two RB 199 afterburner turbofans. The wing has a variable geometry design and double-slot full-span flaps. High-lift devices allow for improved performance and, combined with reverse thrust, allow for landings on short runways. Design began in 1968 and the first of 9 prototypes took flight on August 14, 1974. The first factory-produced airplane took flight on July 10, 1979. The aircraft has an automatic stealth system and a wide range of active and passive self-defense aids.

0.476

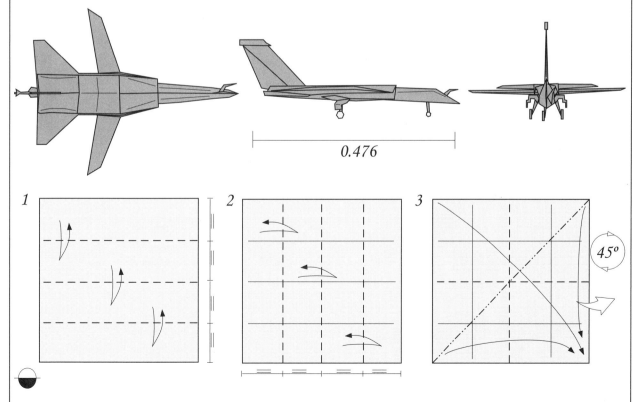

1

2

3

45°

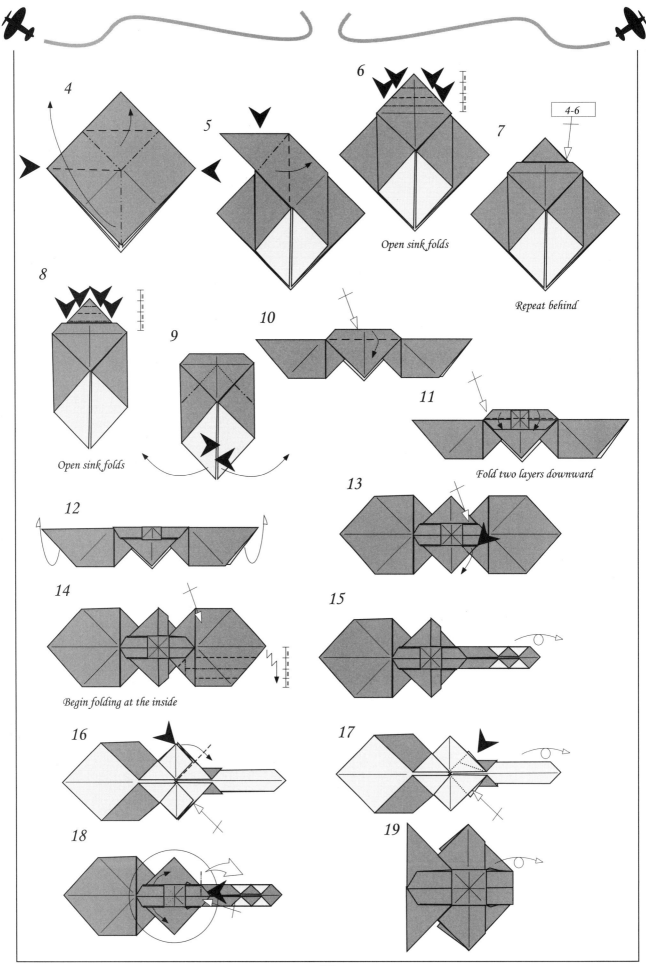

4

5

6

Open sink folds

7

4-6

Repeat behind

8

Open sink folds

9

10

11

Fold two layers downward

12

13

14

Begin folding at the inside

15

16

17

18

19

38

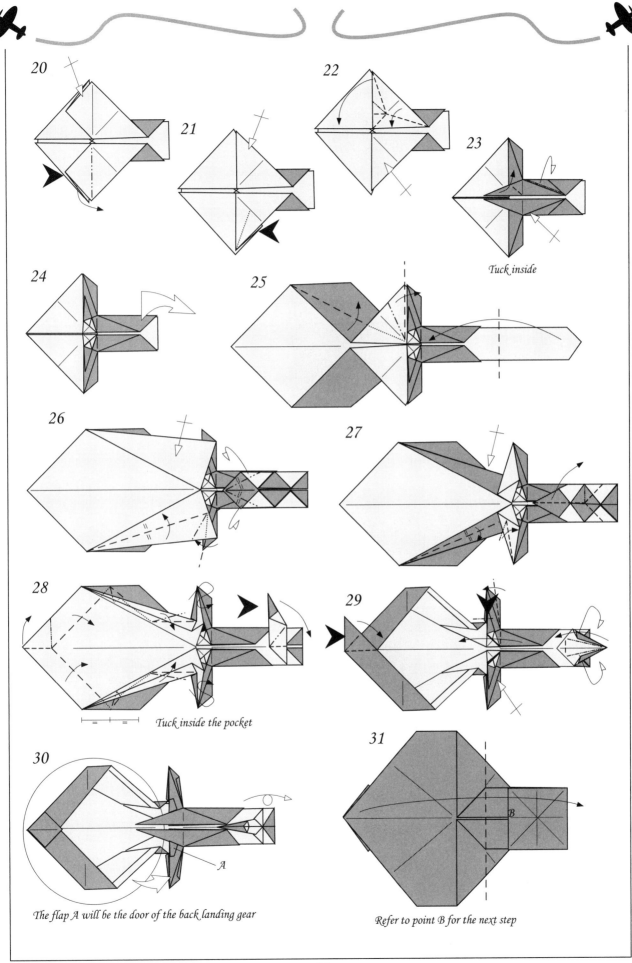

20

21

22

23

Tuck inside

24

25

26

27

28

Tuck inside the pocket

29

30

A

The flap A will be the door of the back landing gear

31

B

Refer to point B for the next step

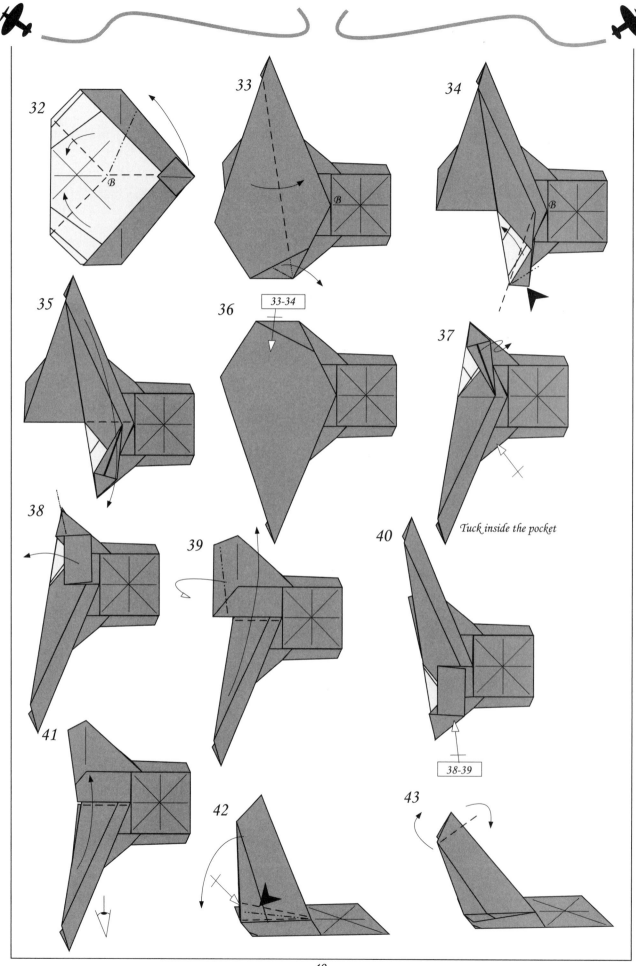

32

33

34

35

36

33-34

37

38

39

40

Tuck inside the pocket

41

42

43

38-39

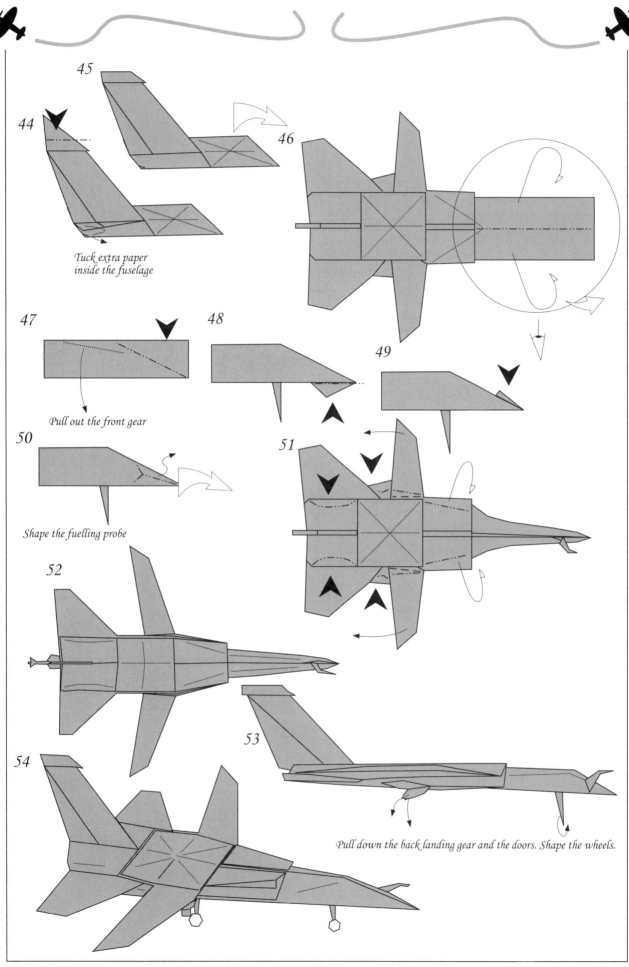

45

44

Tuck extra paper
inside the fuselage

46

47

Pull out the front gear

48

49

50

Shape the fuelling probe

51

52

53

54

Pull down the back landing gear and the doors. Shape the wheels.

F-18
Hornet

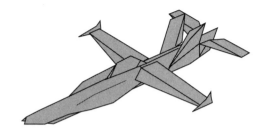

*T*he initial design goal was to make two different versions: the F-18 fighter and the A-18 for attack missions. Later, it was decided that a single version would perform both missions. The new airplane exceeded many expectations when it first entered into service. The F-18 was a genuine multi-mission airplane, with a superior bombing capacity compared to the A-7, and greater agility than the F-14. For the first version, the F/A-18A, a total of 371 airplanes were made and delivered, starting in May of 1980. The first models were used for evaluating the offensive/operational capabilities of the U.S. Marines.

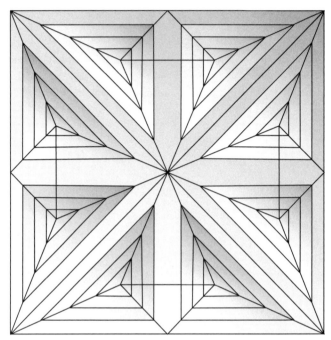

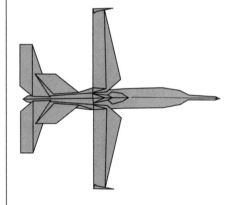

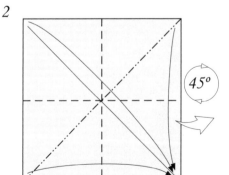

0.571

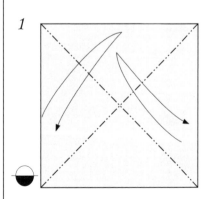

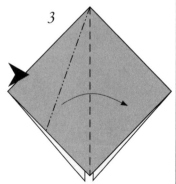

4

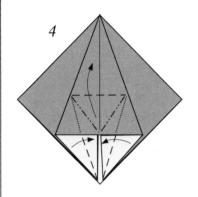

5

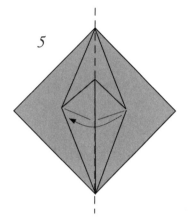

6

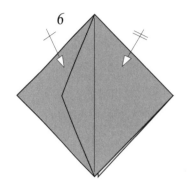

Repeat steps 3 through 5 on the other three corners

7

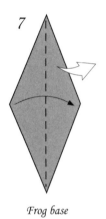

Frog base

8

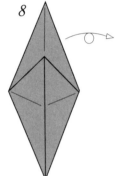

9

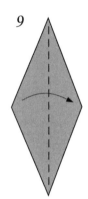

10

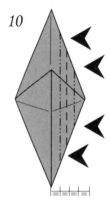

Triple open sink fold

11

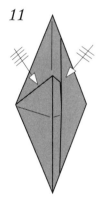

Repeat step 10 on the other 7 flaps

12

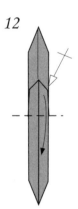

Repeat behind

13

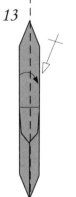

14

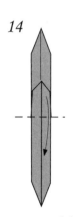

Do not repeat behind

15

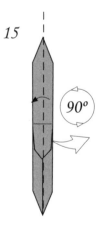

90°

16

17

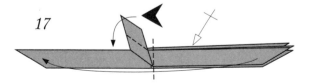

43

18

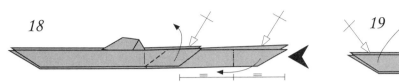

19

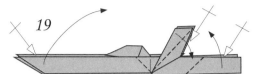

20

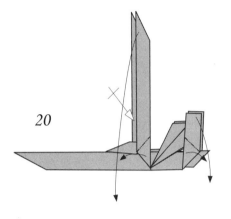

21

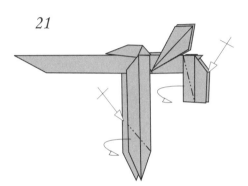

22

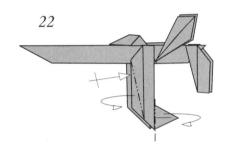

23

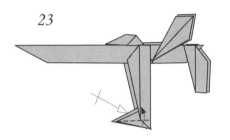

24

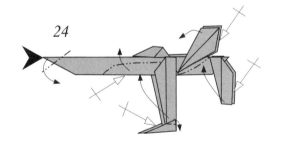

25

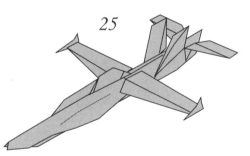

Schweizer-Hughes 300

The Hughes Aircraft Company started to specialize in helicopters in 1948 and its second design proved to be one of the most successful lightweight helicopters in the world. The first of two prototypes (Model 269) took flight in October of 1956. In 1983, production of the 300 C model was turned over to Schweizer. The first model built by this company took flight in 1984, and was followed by the production of many additional versions. These include the TH-300C (for military training, with dual control), the 300 Sky Knight (for police use, has armored seats and a spotlight), and the 300QC (has an extra long tail, is 75% quieter).

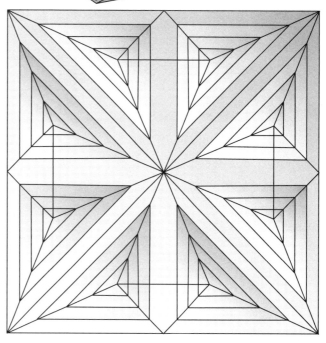

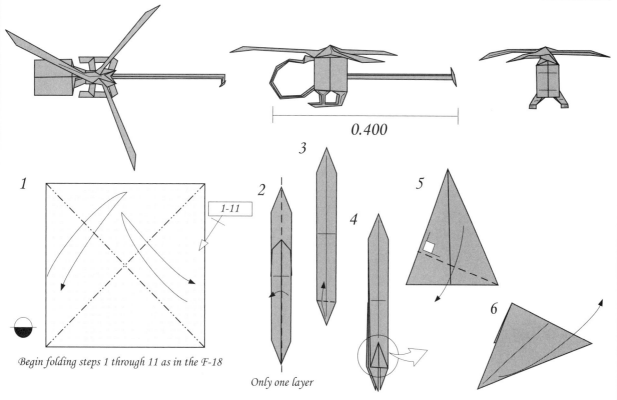

0.400

1

1-11

Begin folding steps 1 through 11 as in the F-18

2

3

4

5

6

Only one layer

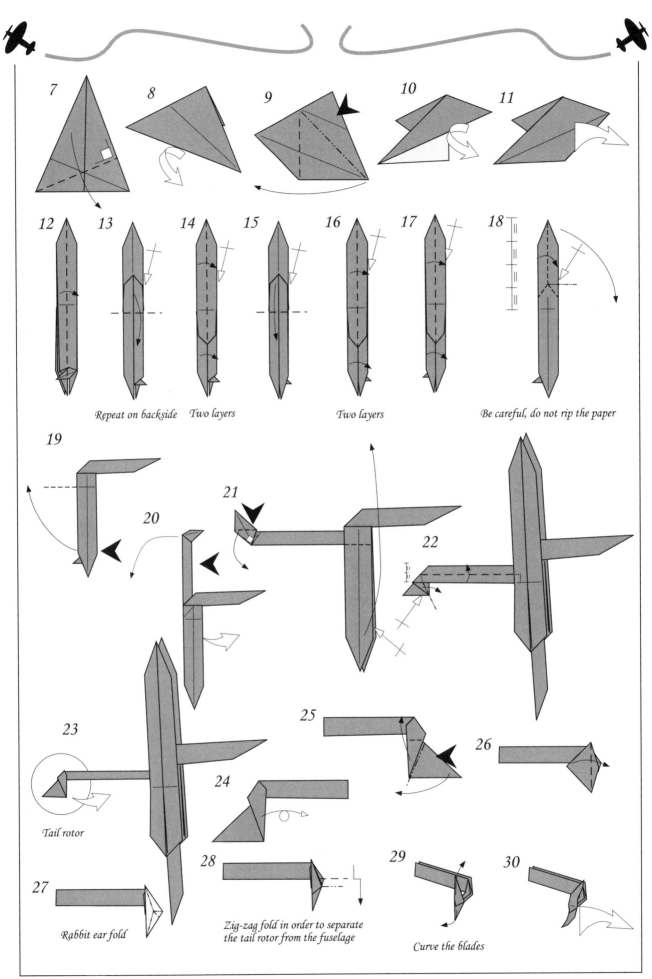

7

8

9

10

11

12

13

14

15

16

17

18

Repeat on backside *Two layers* *Two layers* *Be careful, do not rip the paper*

19

20

21

22

23

Tail rotor

24

25

26

27

Rabbit ear fold

28

Zig-zag fold in order to separate the tail rotor from the fuselage

29

30

Curve the blades

46

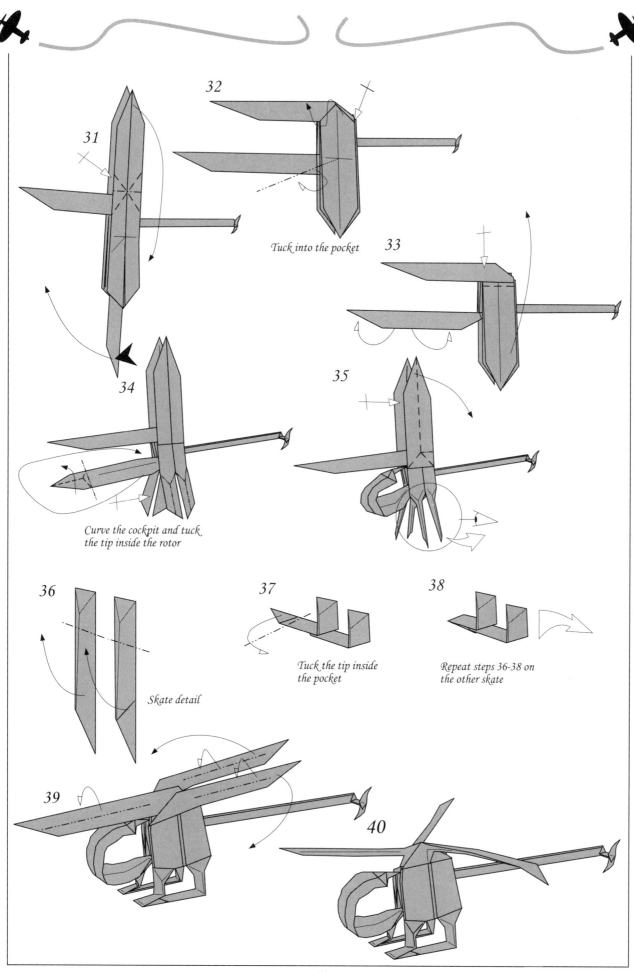

31

32

Tuck into the pocket

33

34

Curve the cockpit and tuck
the tip inside the rotor

35

36

Skate detail

37

Tuck the tip inside
the pocket

38

Repeat steps 36-38 on
the other skate

39

40

Autogyro Cierva C.30

*A*utogyros are different from conventional airplanes in that they are supported in flight by rotating, instead of fixed, wings. Unlike helicopters, the rotor is not powered by an engine. The C.30 represents the peak of Spaniard Juan de la Cierva's life's work. The first prototype was manufactured in 1931. It had a "direct control" system, which changed the rotor angle and made the C.30 fly better than its predecessors—especially during reduced-speed maneuvers and dives. These changes also allowed for shorter takeoffs; only a few years later (1936) runway takeoffs were no longer necessary because of Juan de la Cierva's fine-tuning of the "Autodynamic" rotor, which allowed autogyros to take off with a "jump."

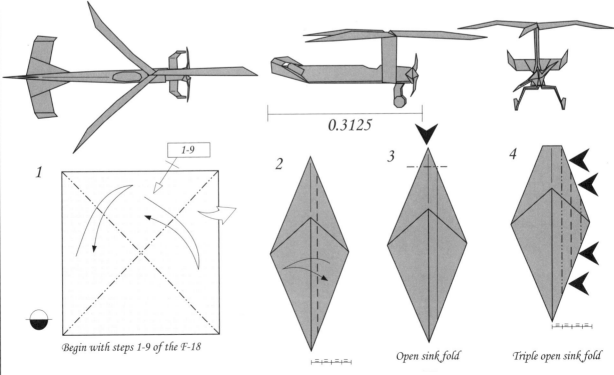

0.3125

1-9

1

Begin with steps 1-9 of the F-18

2

3

Open sink fold

4

Triple open sink fold

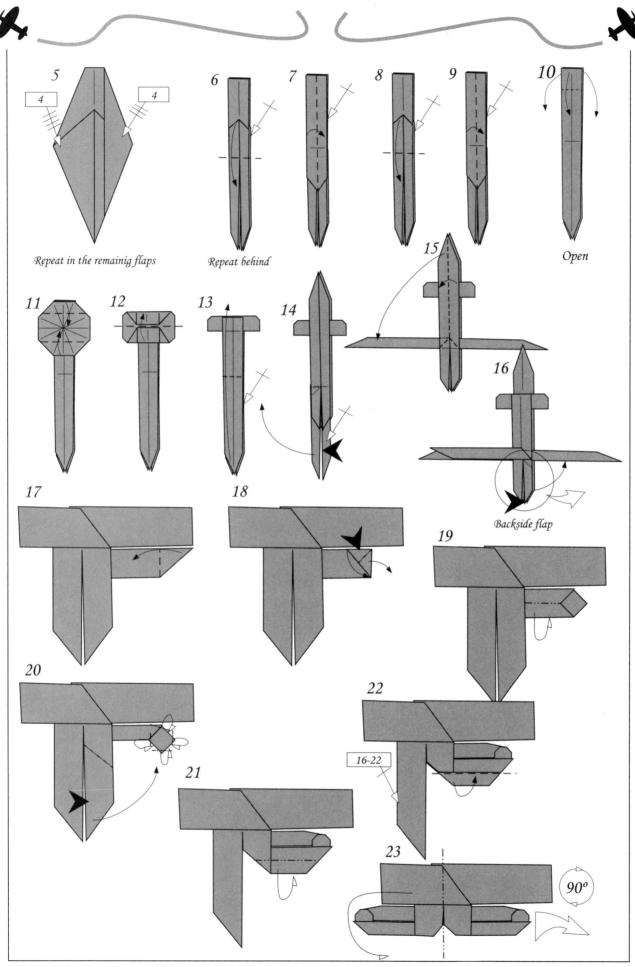

5

4   4

Repeat in the remainig flaps

6   7   8   9   10

Repeat behind   Open

11   12   13   14   15

16

Backside flap

17   18   19

20   21   22

16-22

23   90º

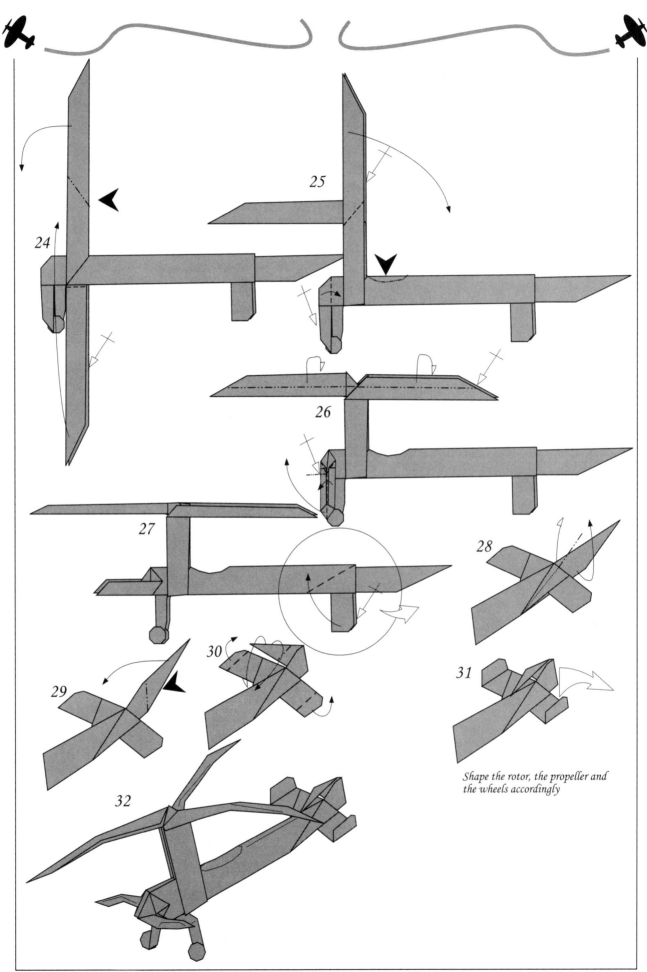

Shape the rotor, the propeller and the wheels accordingly

Autogyro Cierva C.19

*T*his two-seater autogyro was built before the C.30. Manufacturing began in 1929, and during its first public exhibition, was piloted by Juan de la Cierva himself. The tail stabilizer was tilted upwards to deflect the engine slipstream toward the rotor. The rotor was sped up to begin flight, after which the engine was engaged using the clutch. After the rotor reached flying speed, it was left on its own. The autogyro was then able to take off after reaching a ground speed of 15 mph (25 km/hour). This starting procedure prevailed over others that had been used until then.

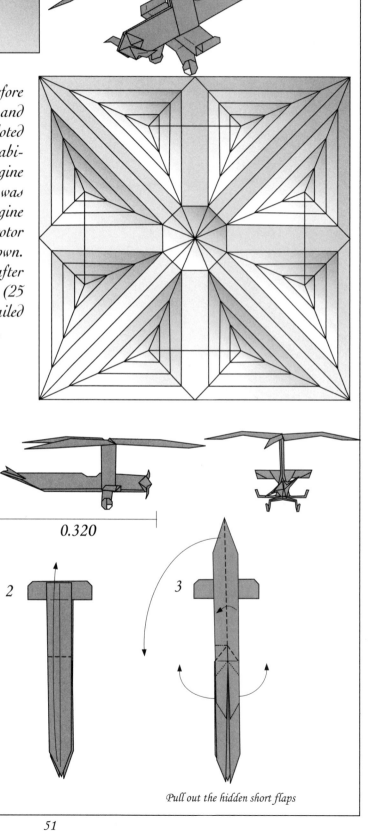

0.320

1-13

1

2

3

Begin with steps 1-13 of the C.30

Pull out the hidden short flaps

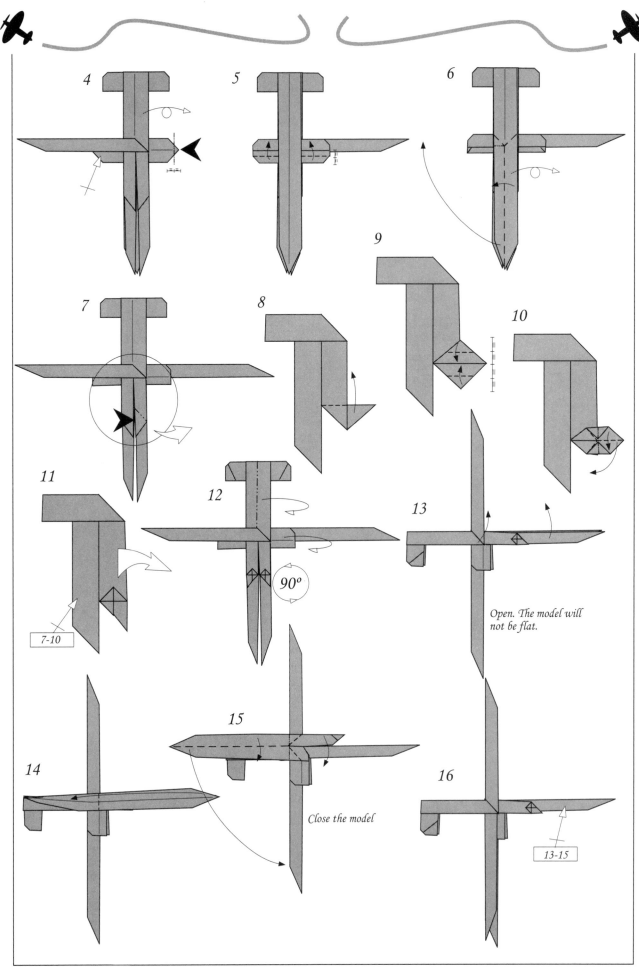

4

5

6

9

7

8

10

11

12

90°

13

Open. The model will not be flat.

7-10

14

15

Close the model

16

13-15

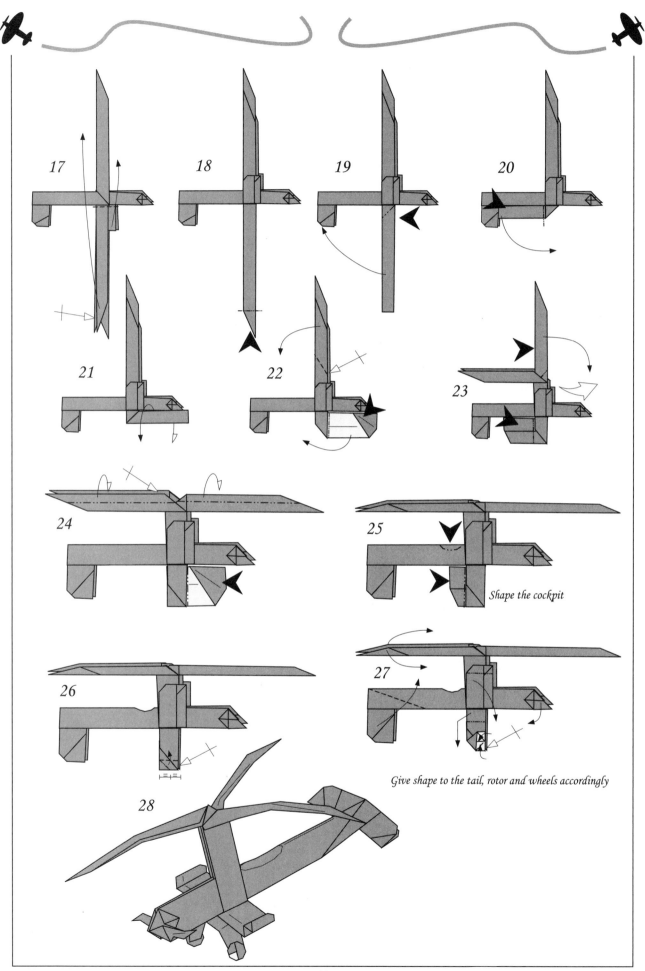

17

18

19

20

21

22

23

24

25

Shape the cockpit

26

27

Give shape to the tail, rotor and wheels accordingly

28

Eurofighter Typhoon

Following up on the Tornado program, the Eurofighter partnership was established in June of 1986 between Great Britain, Germany, Italy, and Spain. The airplane has an aerodynamically unstable configuration, canard plans, a digital active control system called "fly-by-wire," and complex avionics features. It was made of carbon fiber materials and aluminum-lithium and titanium alloys. The first two prototypes, the DA.1 and the DA.2, took flight in 1994. Both had provisional RB.199-22 turbofans. The DA.3 was the first model to fly with the benchmark EJ200 engines. Each engine has a dry thrust of 60 kN and an afterburner thrust of 90 kN. Future versions may incorporate vector thrust nozzles.

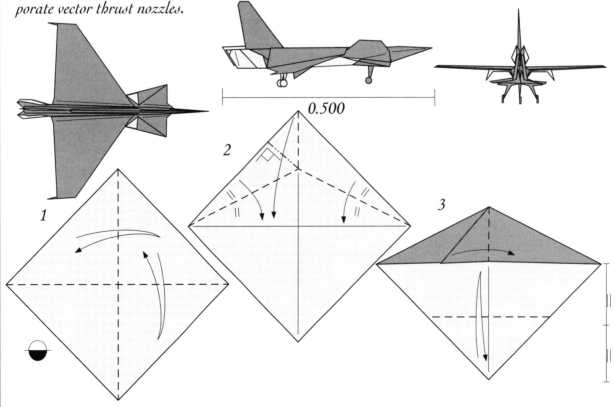

0.500

1

2

3

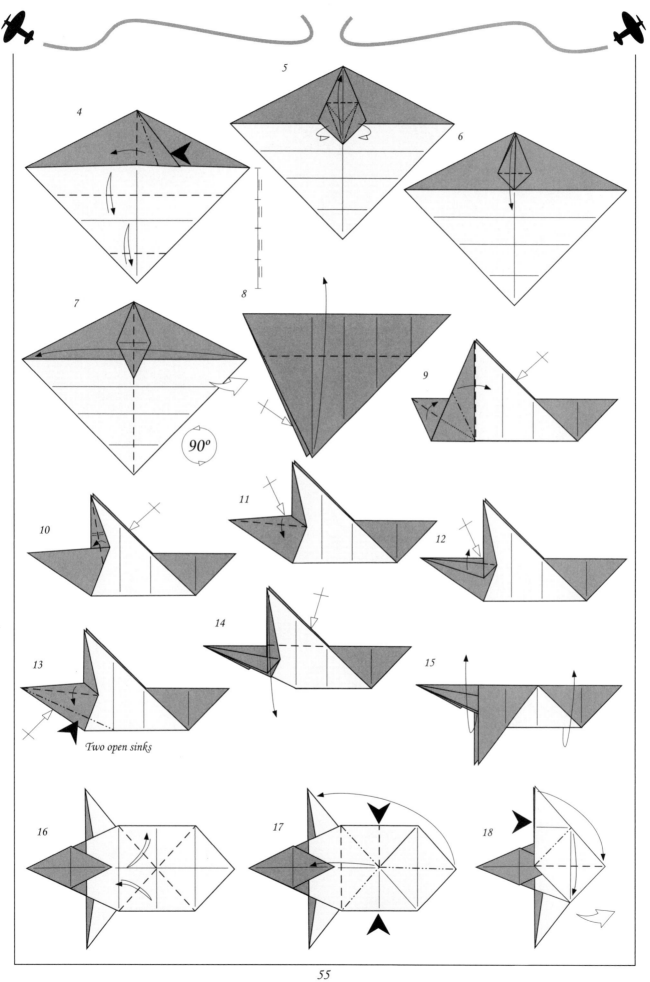

4

5

6

7

8

9

90°

10

11

12

13

Two open sinks

14

15

16

17

18

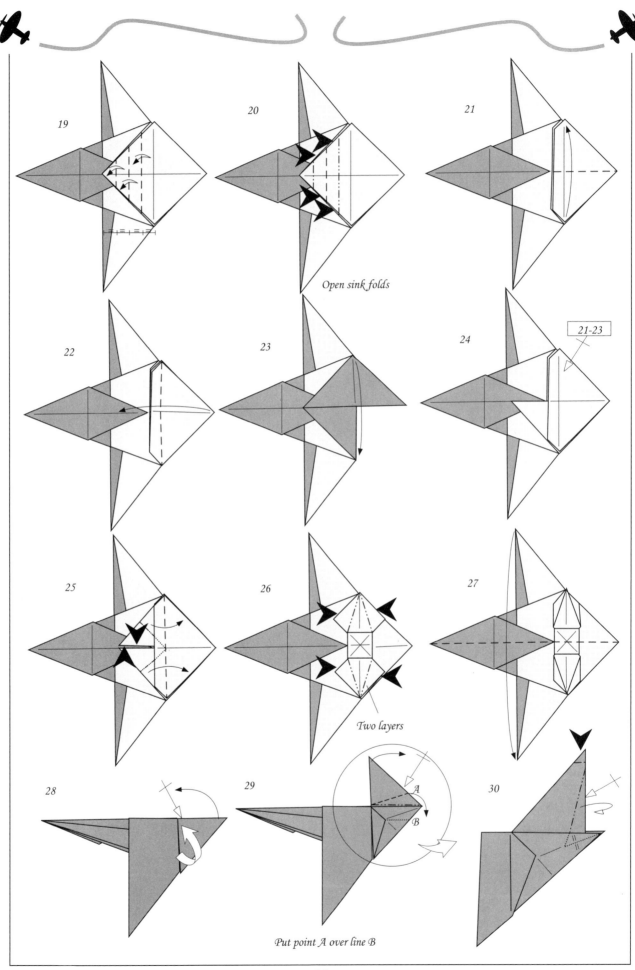

19

20

Open sink folds

21

22

23

24

21-23

25

26

Two layers

27

28

29

Put point A over line B

A

B

30

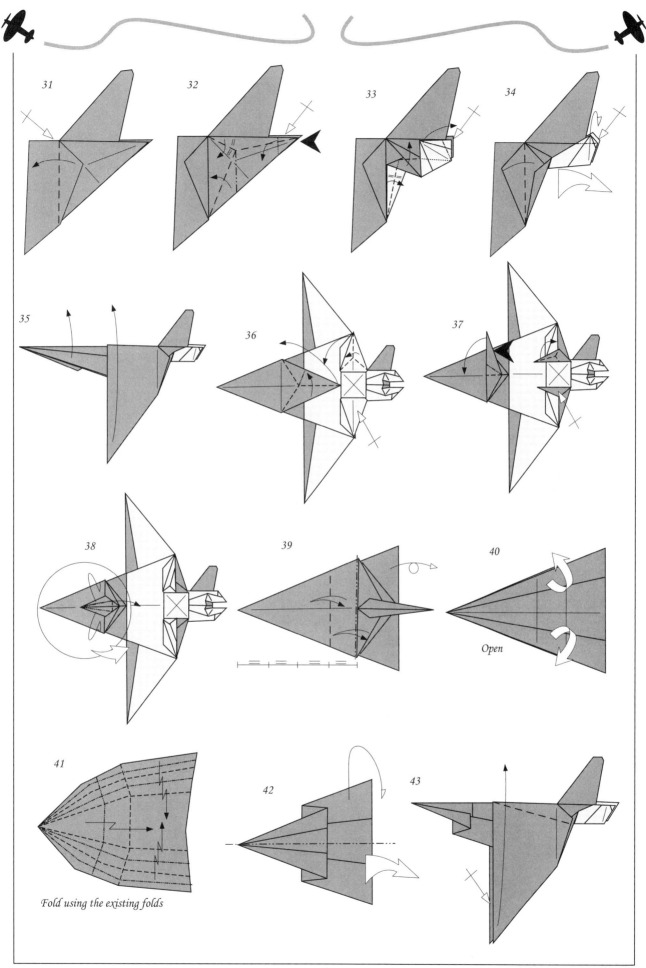

31

32

33

34

35

36

37

38

39

40

Open

41

Fold using the existing folds

42

43

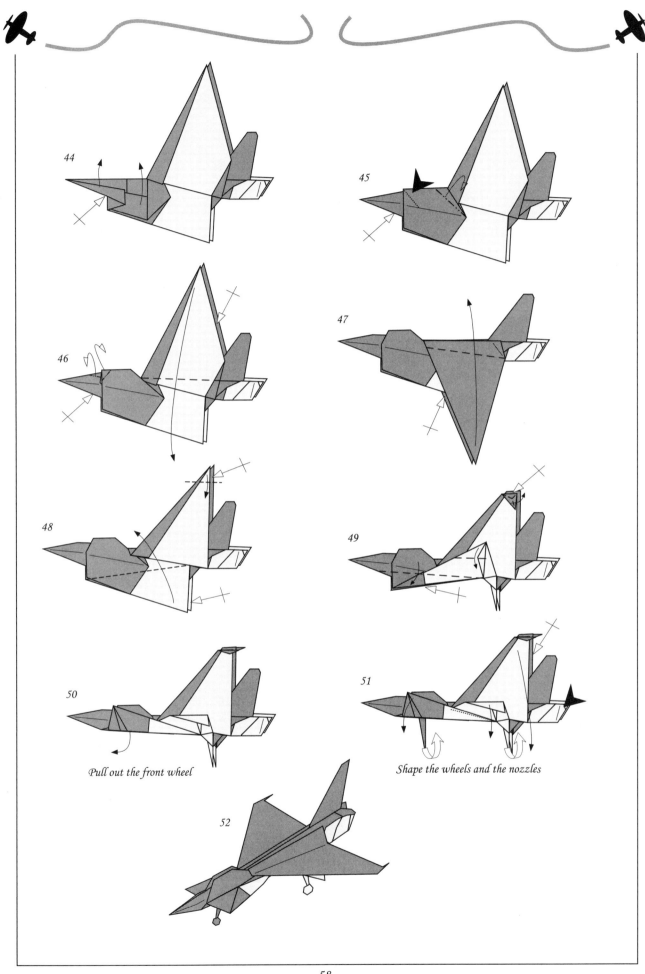

44

45

46

47

48

49

50

Pull out the front wheel

51

Shape the wheels and the nozzles

52

McDonnell Douglas MD-80

This family of civilian twin-engine airplanes, derived from the DC-9, has experienced the greatest amount of change in the history of commercial planes. The first airplane, the DC-9, had 80 seats and a 104-foot (32-meter) fuselage. It went into service in December of 1965. The design evolved until the MD-90 was developed, with its more powerful engines, longer fuselage (152.5 feet / 46.5 meters), and capacity for 187 passengers. Over 2,400 DC-9s and subsequent models have been sold during the past 30 years. New versions, called MD-95s, continue to be manufactured. They are also known as Boeing 717s.

0.610

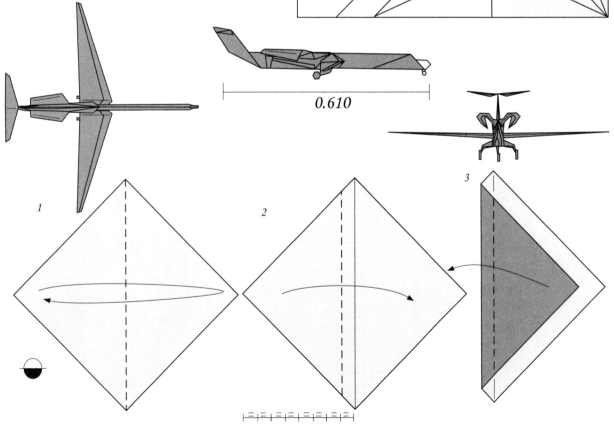

1

2

3

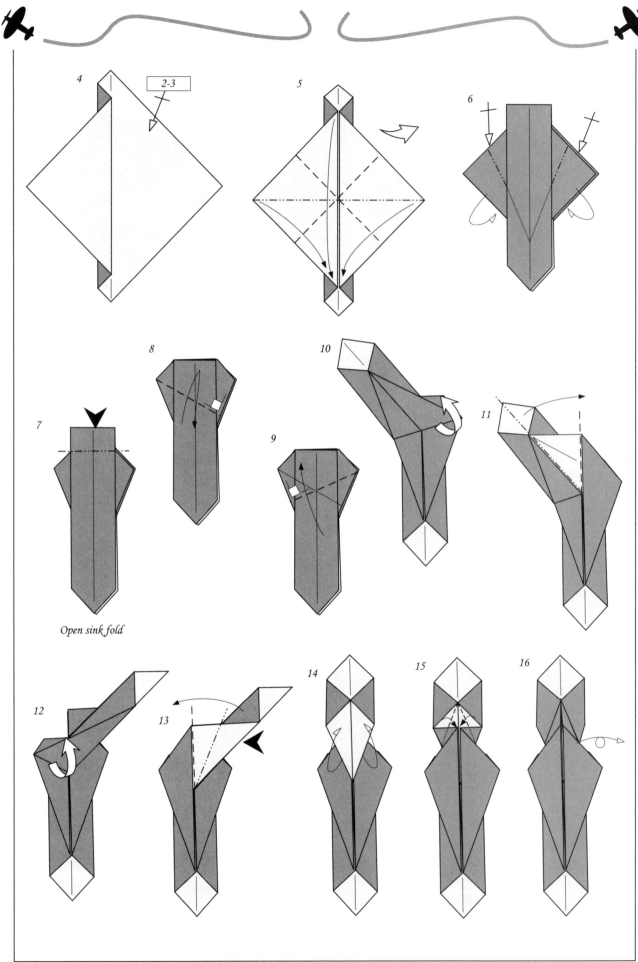

Open sink fold

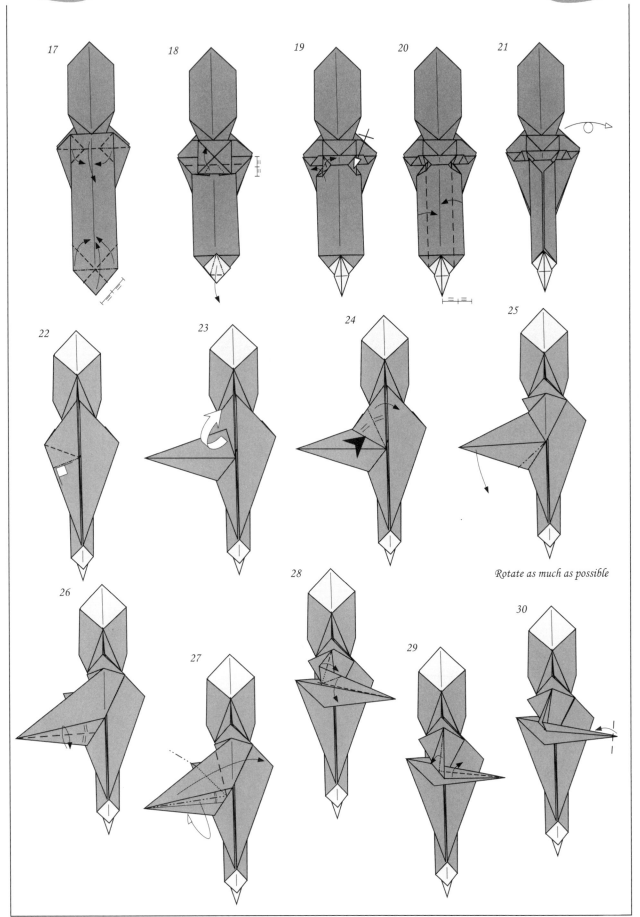

17

18

19

20

21

22

23

24

25

Rotate as much as possible

26

27

28

29

30

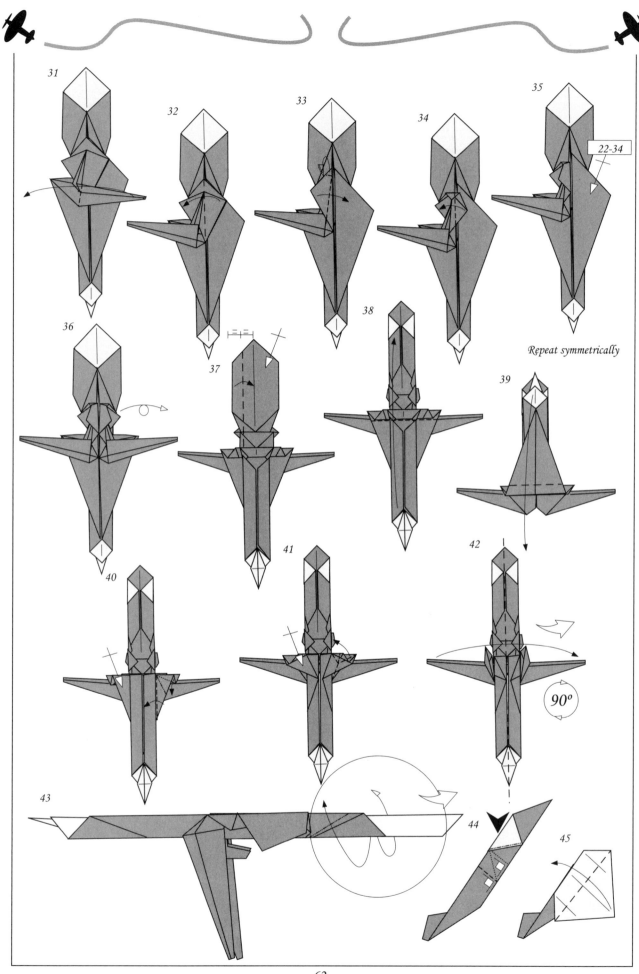

31

32

33

34

35

22-34

36

37

38

Repeat symmetrically

39

40

41

42

90°

43

44

45

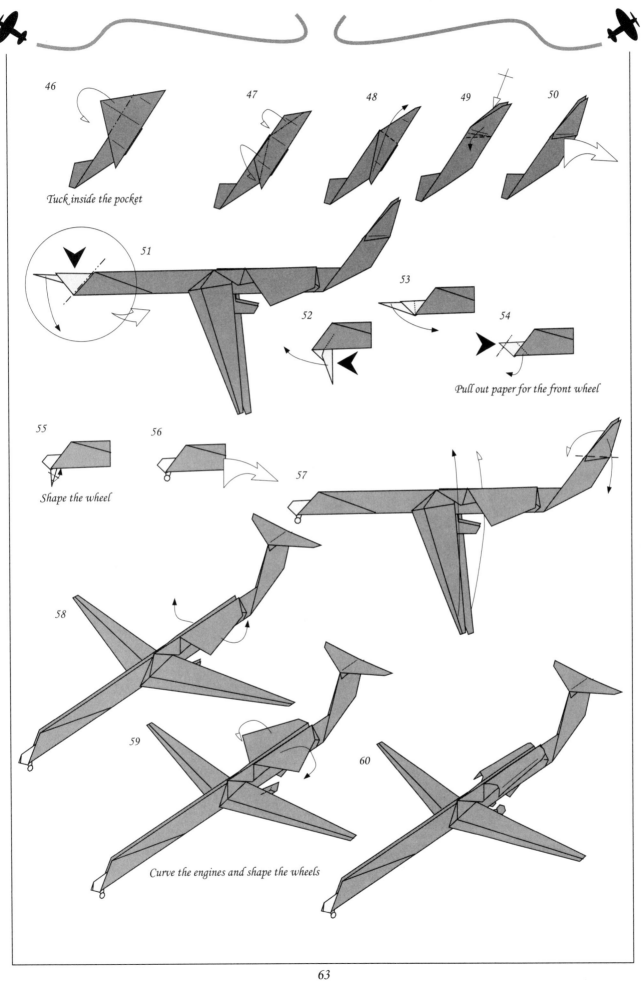

46

Tuck inside the pocket

47

48

49

50

51

52

53

54

Pull out paper for the front wheel

55

Shape the wheel

56

57

58

59

Curve the engines and shape the wheels

60

C-212
Aviocar

This model was developed as a STOL ("short take off and landing") airplane to replace the DC-3 and Junkers JU-52 airplanes in the Spanish Air Force. The first prototype took flight in March of 1971. It was designed to be a military airplane, although the first civilian versions, called C-212C, were delivered in July of 1975. Although military production was discontinued in 1975 (after 260 units were manufactured), commercial versions were developed that included significant engine and wing configuration improvements that greatly enhanced performance.

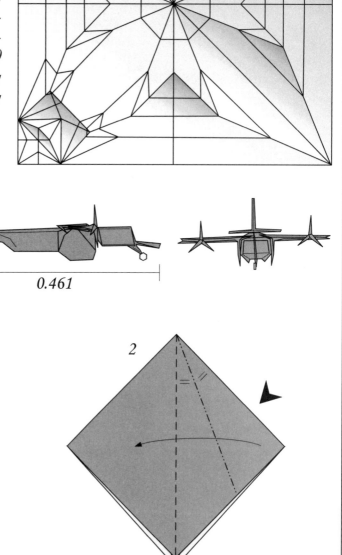

0.461

1

2

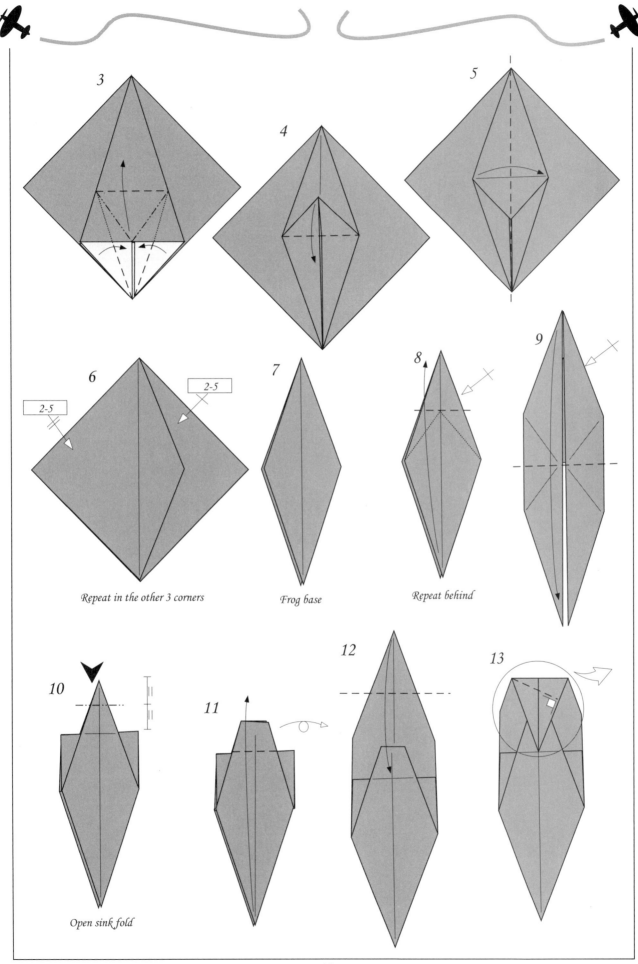

3

4

5

6

2-5

2-5

Repeat in the other 3 corners

7

Frog base

8

Repeat behind

9

10

Open sink fold

11

12

13

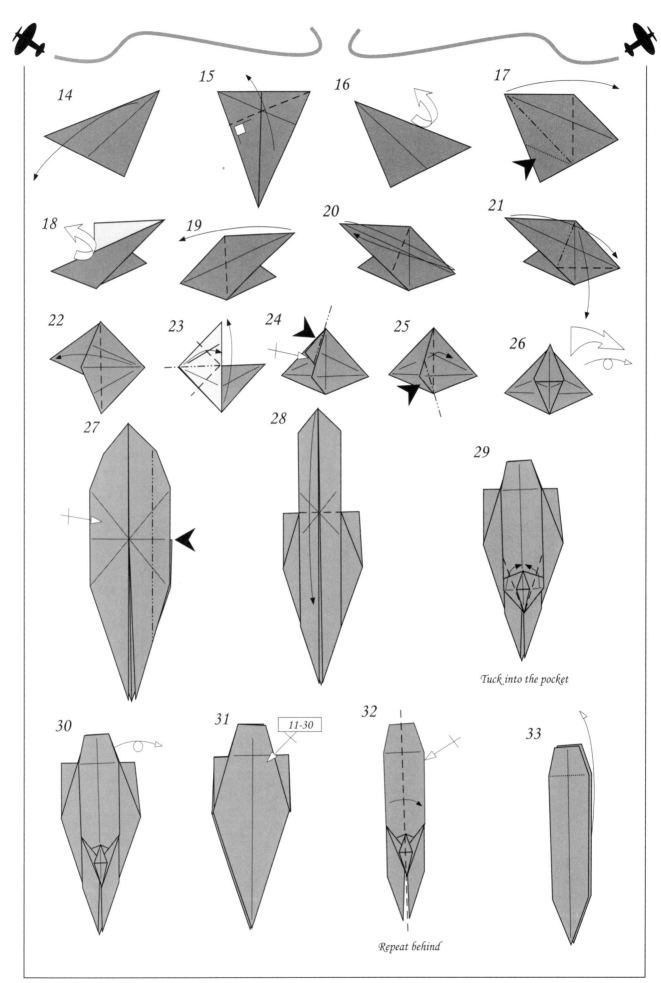

14

15

16

17

18

19

20

21

22

23

24

25

26

27

28

29

Tuck into the pocket

30

31

11-30

32

33

Repeat behind

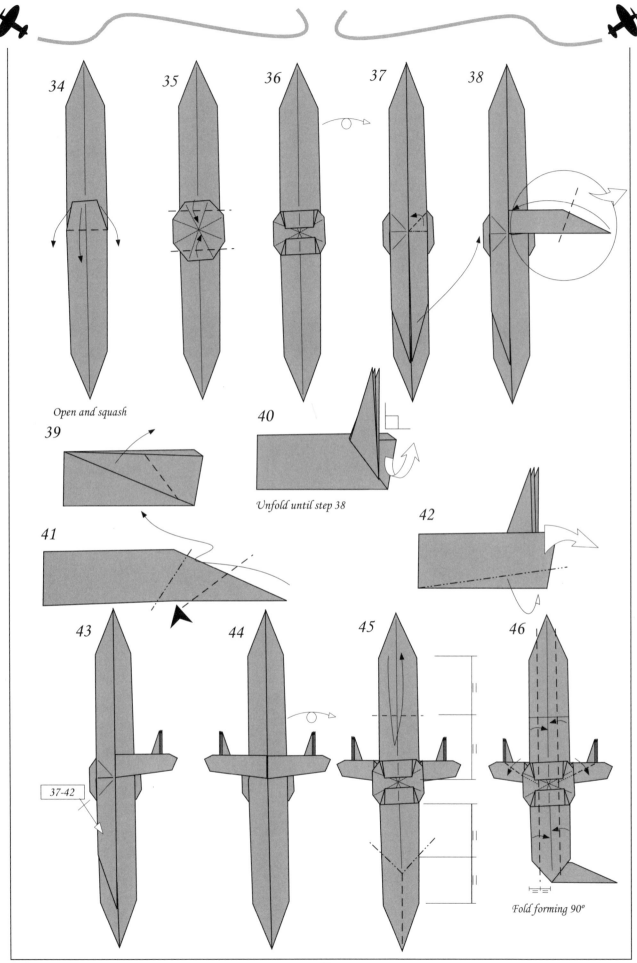

34

35

36

37

38

Open and squash

39

40

Unfold until step 38

41

42

43

37-42

44

45

46

Fold forming 90°

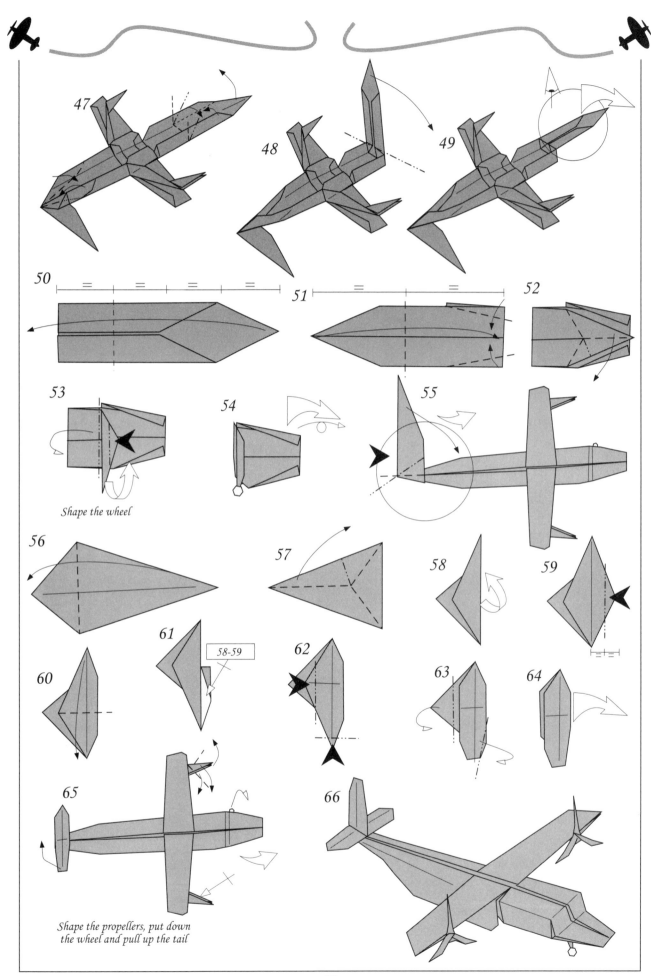

47

48

49

50

51

52

53

Shape the wheel

54

55

56

57

58

59

60

61

58-59

62

63

64

65

Shape the propellers, put down
the wheel and pull up the tail

66

Bell/Boeing V-22 Osprey

The V-22 Osprey combined the lift capabilities of a helicopter and the great speed and efficiency of a fixed-wing airplane. The airplane is propelled by two Allison 6150 shp turboshaft engines placed at the tips of the wings, which move three-bladed proprotors using cross-coupled transmissions, and are located in gondolas capable of rotating up to 97.5°. The first prototype flight occurred in Texas in March of 1989. In September, the V-22 was the first aircraft to change from helicopter to fixed-wing flight. The crew consists of a pilot, a copilot and a crew chief. Twenty-four soldiers and 12 berths or internal loads can fit in the cabin

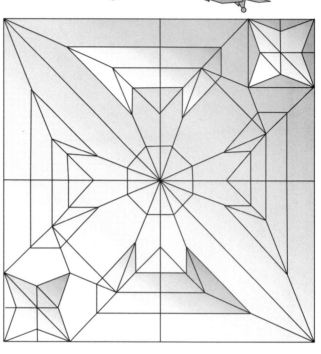

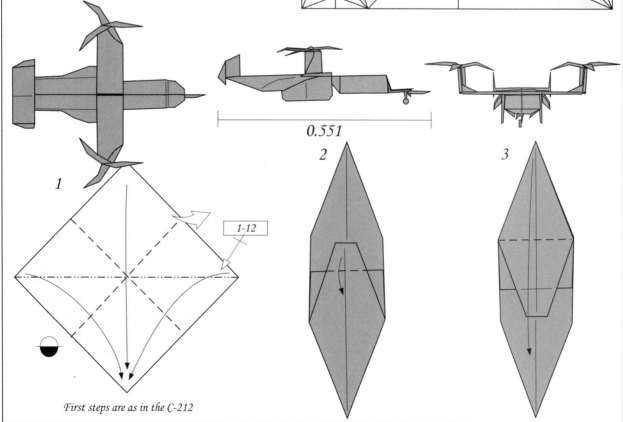

0.551

1

2

3

1-12

First steps are as in the C-212

69

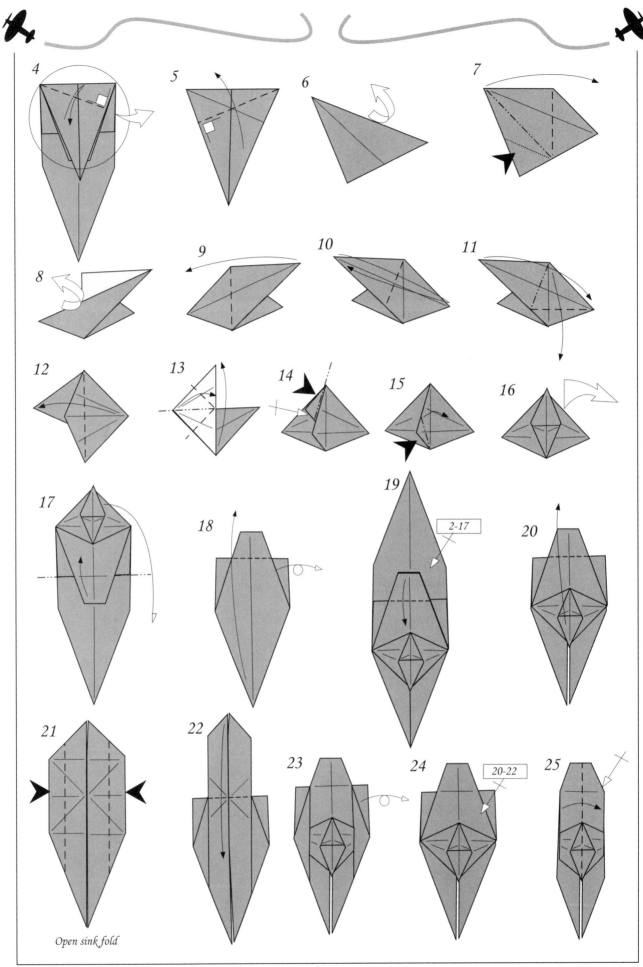

4

5

6

7

8

9

10

11

12

13

14

15

16

17

18

19

2-17

20

21

22

23

24

20-22

25

Open sink fold

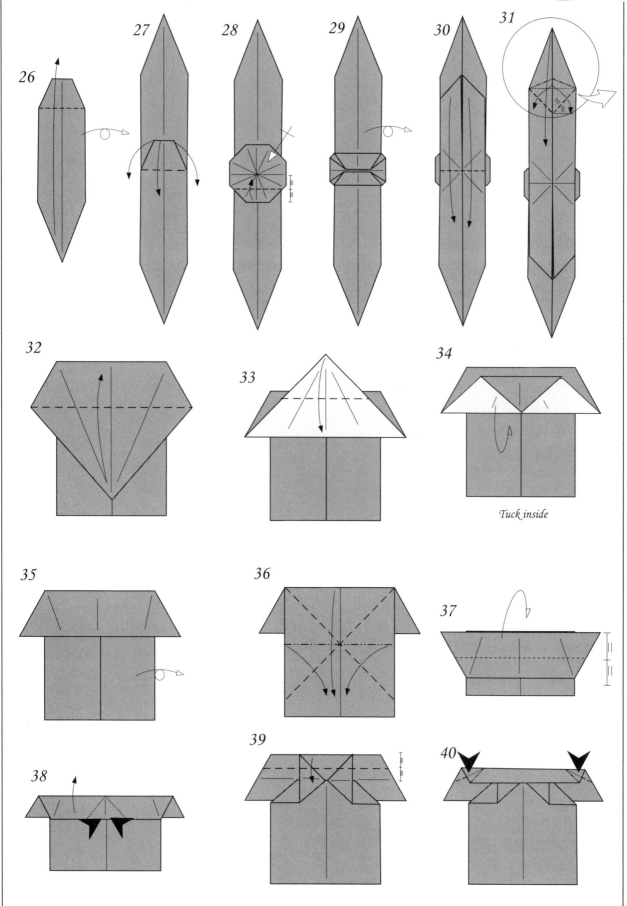

26

27

28

29

30

31

32

33

34

Tuck inside

35

36

37

38

39

40

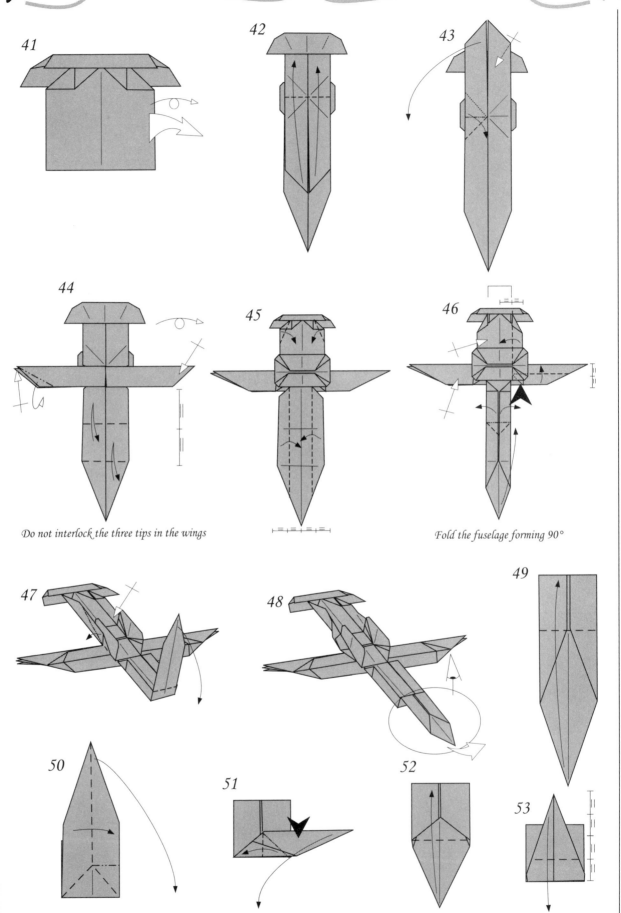

41

42

43

44

Do not interlock the three tips in the wings

45

46

Fold the fuselage forming 90°

47

48

49

50

51

52

53

54

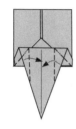

55

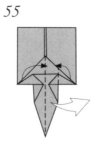

Fold forming 90°

56

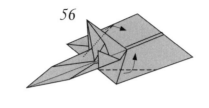

57

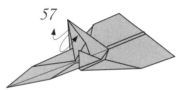

Shape the front wheel

58

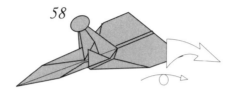

59

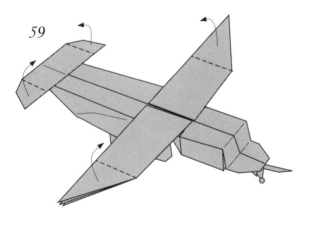

60

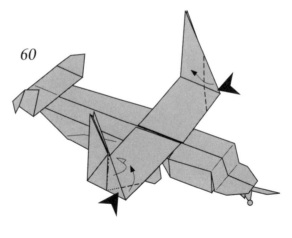

61

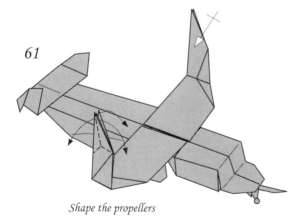

Shape the propellers

62

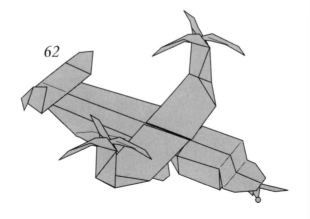

Fokker Dr. I
The Red Baron

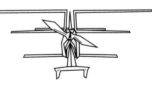

This triplane is perhaps the most famous World War I German fighter because it was used by aces like Manfred von Richthofen. The airplane's speed and fast climb are legendary. Designers were inspired by the Sopwith Triplane and made changes to the three-wing model to maximize surface area and minimize wingspan. It had a rotating engine designed by Reinhold Pfalz, a steel tubing fuselage, and cantilever-like wings, a wooden structure and laminated attack edges. It went into service in August of 1917. Four-hundred and twenty airplanes had been manufactured by the time production ceased in May of 1918.

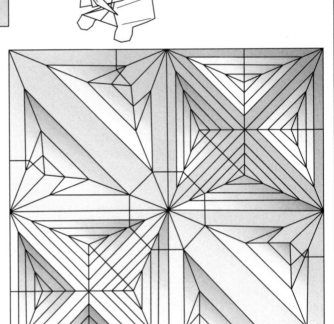

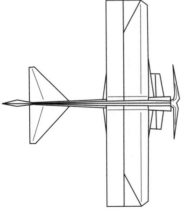

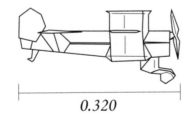

0.320

1

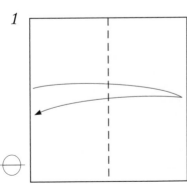

2

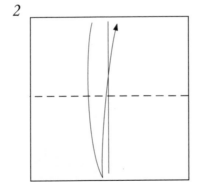

3

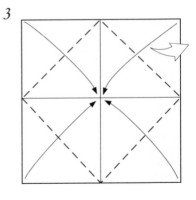

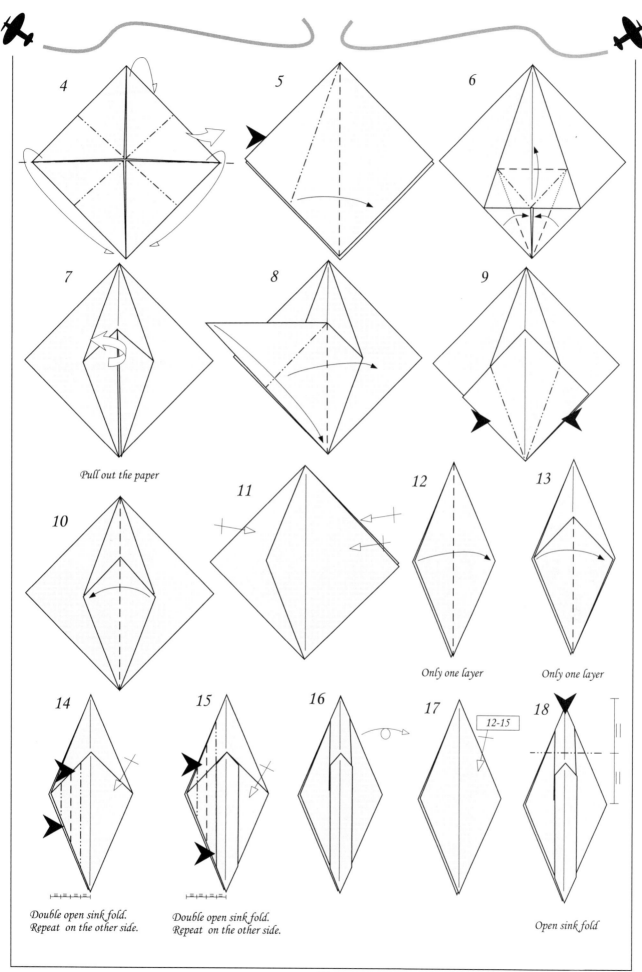

4

5

6

7

Pull out the paper

8

9

10

11

12

Only one layer

13

Only one layer

14

Double open sink fold.
Repeat on the other side.

15

Double open sink fold.
Repeat on the other side.

16

17

12-15

18

Open sink fold

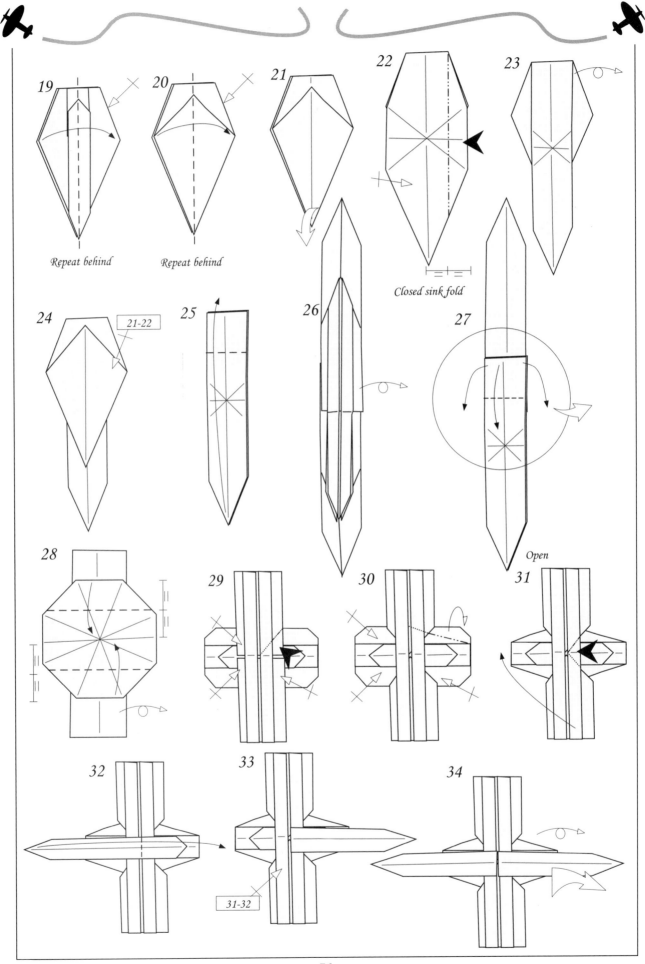

19

20

21

Repeat behind

Repeat behind

22

Closed sink fold

23

24

21-22

25

26

27

Open

28

29

30

31

32

33

31-32

34

76

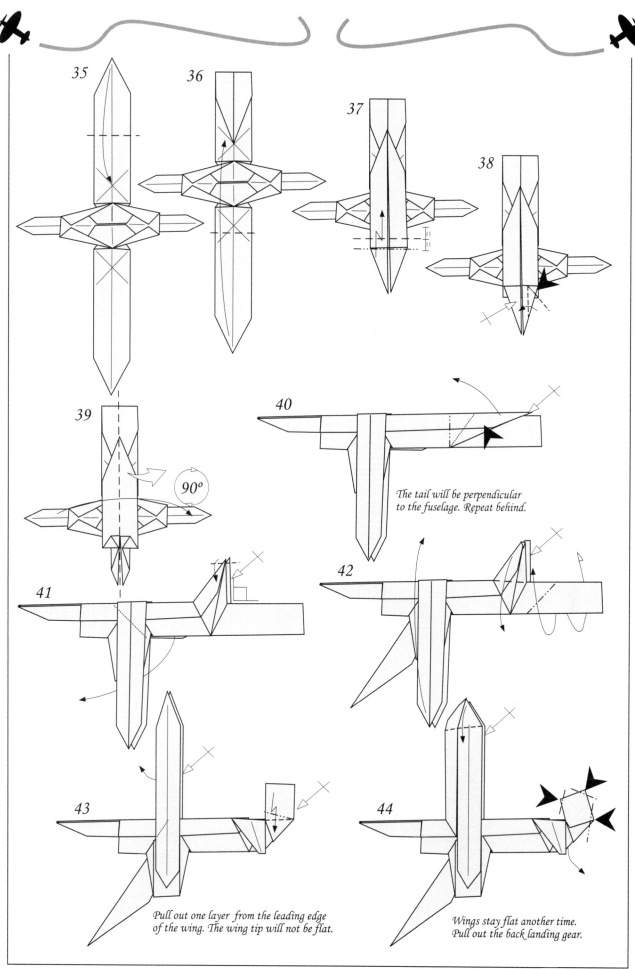

35

36

37

38

39

90°

40

The tail will be perpendicular
to the fuselage. Repeat behind.

41

42

43

Pull out one layer from the leading edge
of the wing. The wing tip will not be flat.

44

Wings stay flat another time.
Pull out the back landing gear.

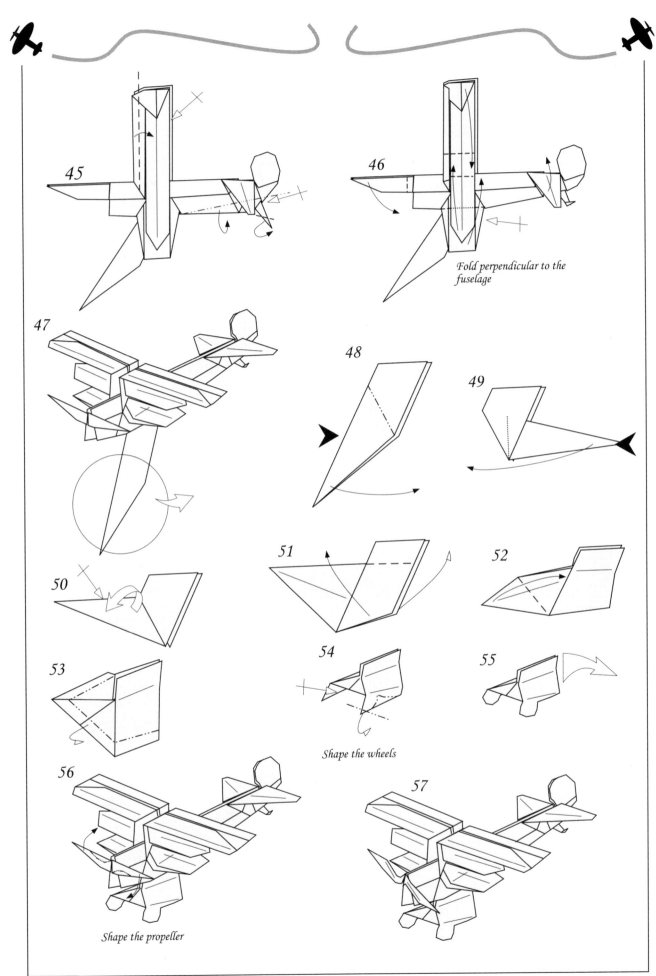

45

46

Fold perpendicular to the
fuselage

47

48

49

50

51

52

53

54

Shape the wheels

55

56

Shape the propeller

57

Sopwith F.1 Camel

Based on the number of airplanes it destroyed (1,294), the Camel was the best allied fighter plane in World War I. Derived from the Pup, it went into service in 1917. Its nickname, the "Camel," referred to the bulging fuselage where the machine guns were placed. The bulk of the airplane's mass was located in the fuselage's prow, which gave this fighter plane great speed, although inexperienced pilots had a hard time turning the airplane. A naval version, the 2F.1, was also manufactured with a single machine gun, a smaller wingspan, and removable tail. Total Camel production totaled 5,490 airplanes.

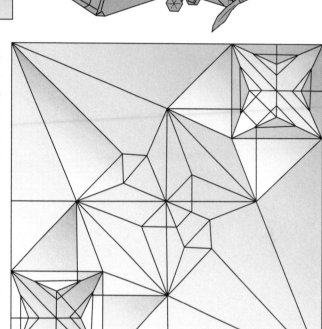

0.260

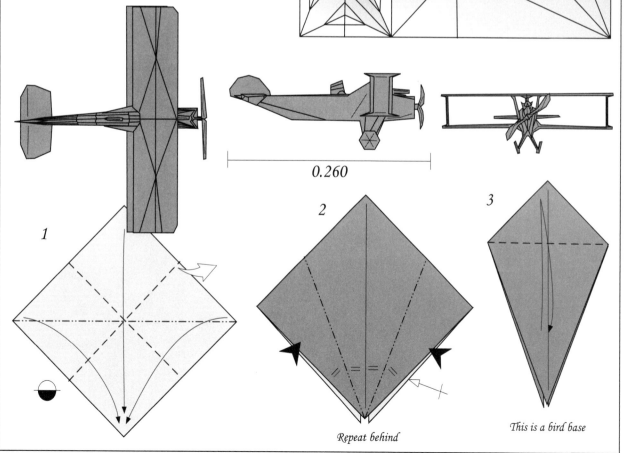

1

2

Repeat behind

3

This is a bird base

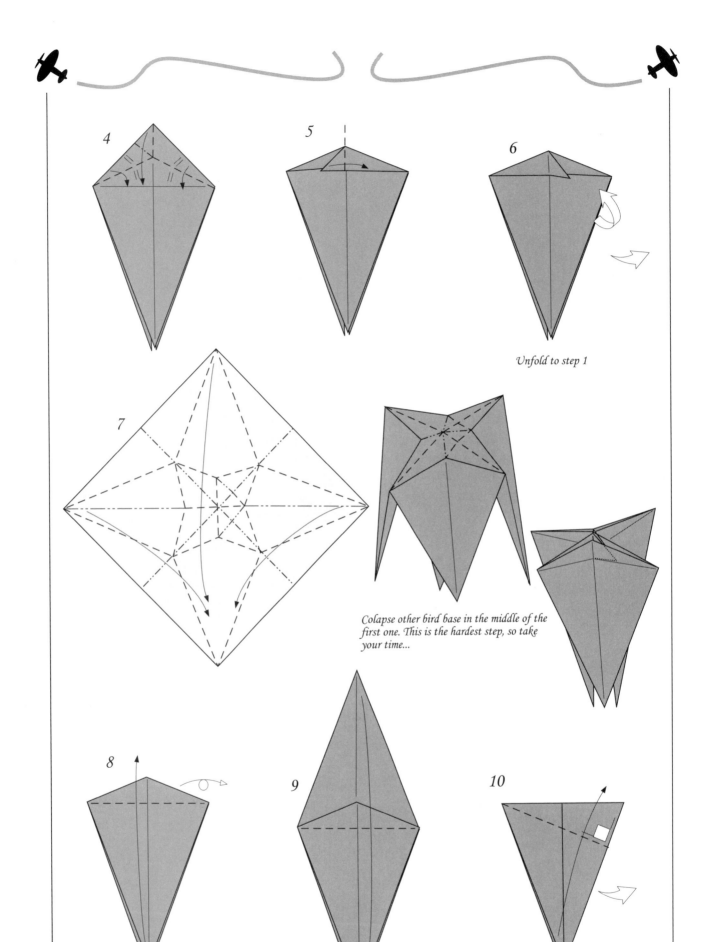

4

5

6

Unfold to step 1

7

Colapse other bird base in the middle of the first one. This is the hardest step, so take your time...

8

9

10

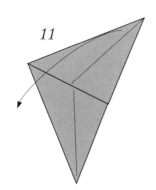

11

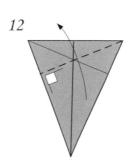

12

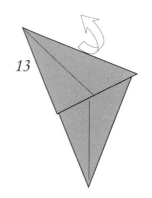

13

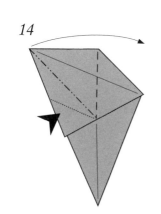

14

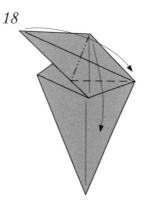

15

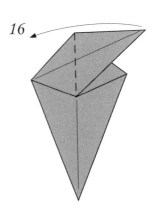

16

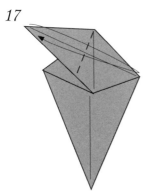

17

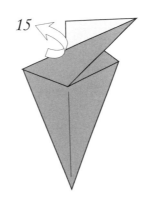

18

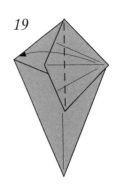

19

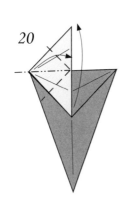

20

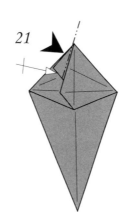

21

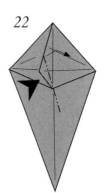

22

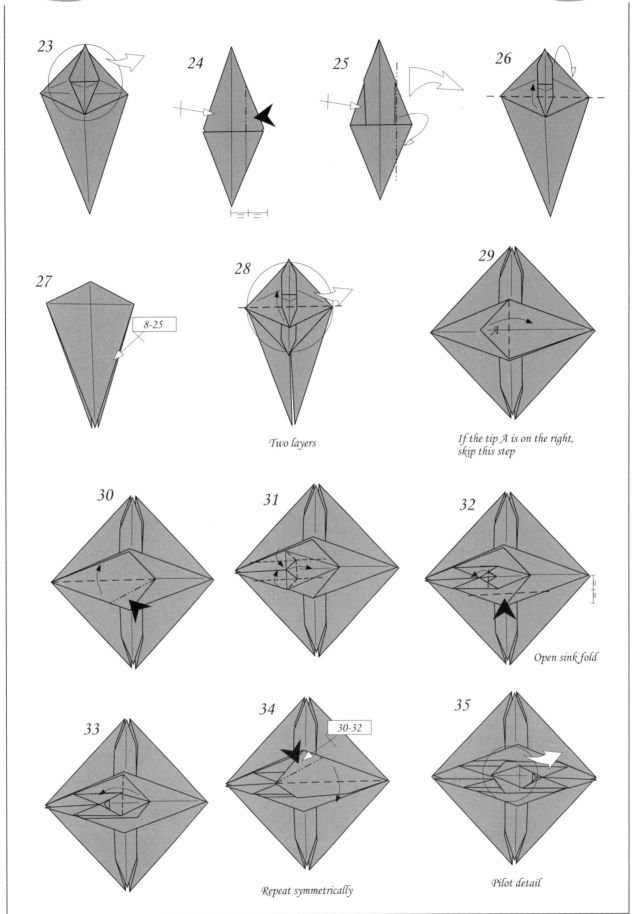

23

24

25

26

27

8-25

28

Two layers

29

A

If the tip A is on the right,
skip this step

30

31

32

Open sink fold

33

34

30-32

35

Repeat symmetrically

Pilot detail

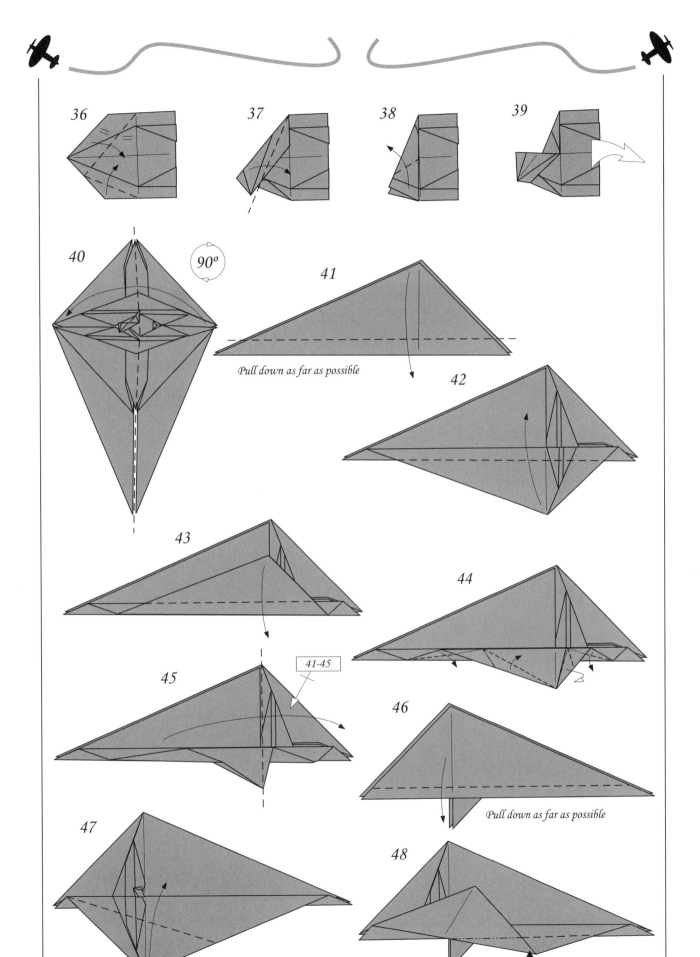

36

37

38

39

40

90°

41

Pull down as far as possible

42

43

44

45

41-45

46

Pull down as far as possible

47

48

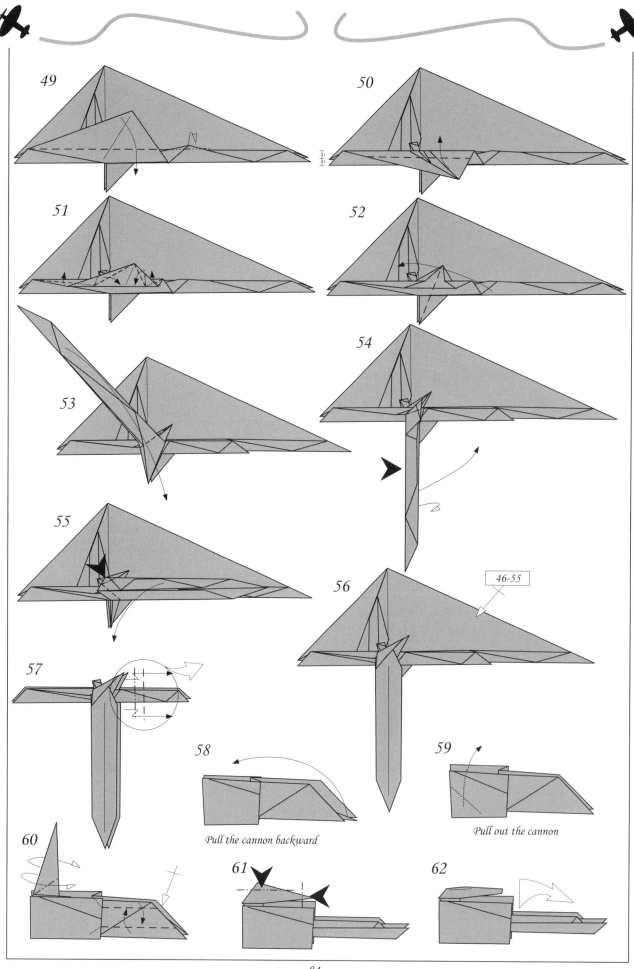

49

50

51

52

53

54

55

56

46-55

57

58

Pull the cannon backward

59

Pull out the cannon

60

61

62

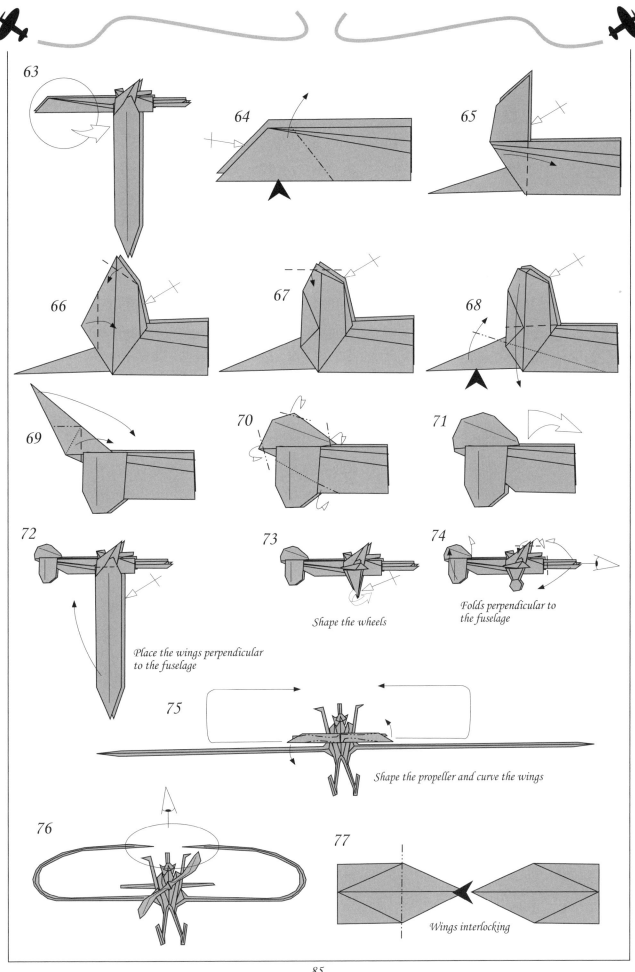

63

64

65

66

67

68

69

70

71

72

Place the wings perpendicular
to the fuselage

73

Shape the wheels

74

Folds perpendicular to
the fuselage

75

Shape the propeller and curve the wings

76

77

Wings interlocking

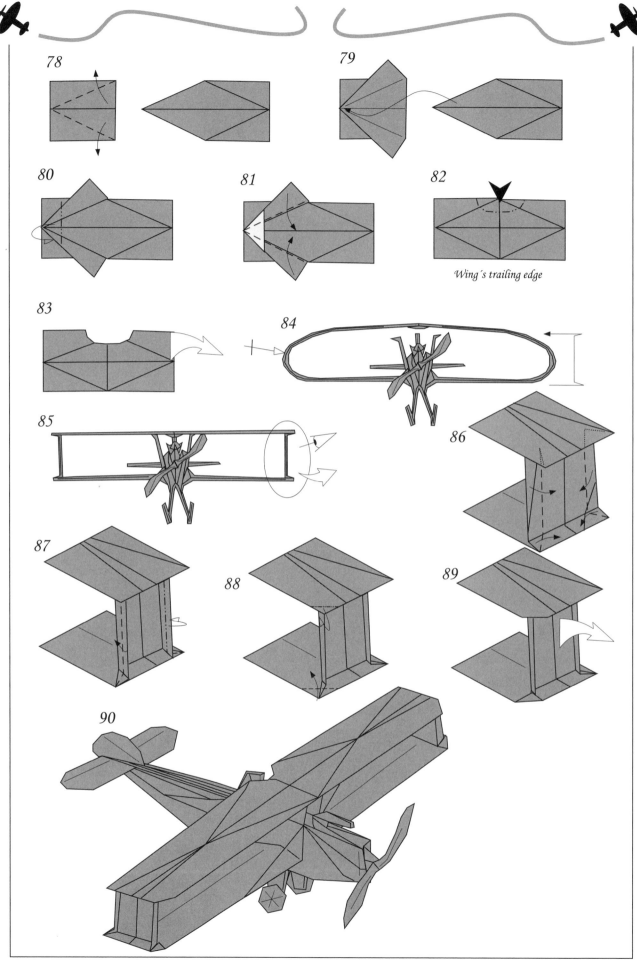

78

79

80

81

82

Wing's trailing edge

83

84

85

86

87

88

89

90

Techniques, Insignias, and Finishing Touches

In this section, I will give you several tips on how to add a few finishing touches to the models. However, keep in mind that these are only suggestions. Do not hesitate to try out new techniques.

First off, we have to focus on choosing the paper. The first few models in this book are simpler, so they can be folded using almost any type of paper. I have even folded the F-117 and A320 using thin cardboard. For the later models, I would recommend metallic foil paper. This paper holds shapes really well and will not unfold. The only negative is that it is hard to reverse the folds (from a mountain to a valley). One side is white and the other is shiny. There are several colors available: silver, gold, blue, green, red, etc.

A technique I use quite often in my figures includes the use of "sandwich paper." We glue tissue paper to metallic foil. This way, we get the color we want (tissue paper comes in a wide variety of colors), while enjoying the advantages of the foil. I use glue sticks, but other people prefer spray adhesives. Since tissue paper is so thin, we can vary its final shade by gluing the tissue paper to either the white or shiny foil side.

Enough about paper. Let's talk about the models. I suggest that you get ahold of pictures of the finished models and study the colors, insignias, details, etc. Depending on the level of realism you want to achieve, you can choose among several techniques.

For some models, choosing a good color is enough. For example, for the F-117, you can get good results if you use black sandwich paper. Once we get into multiple colors with other models, we will have to pay attention to both sides of the paper. Such is the case with the Space Shuttle (black and white), the glider (white and blue) and the Eurofighter (black and grey.)

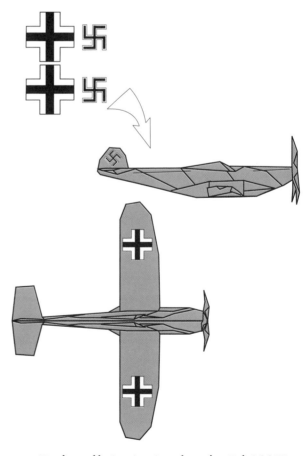

Luftwaffe insignias for the Bf 109K

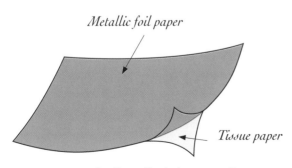

Metallic foil paper

Tissue paper

How to make "sandwich paper"

One additional step to improve the model is to add details or insignias. This is not done very often, but is a simple way to improve the final look of the model. For example, we can add Luftwaffe insignias to the wings and tail of the Messerschmitt Bf 109K. Insignias can be painted on a sheet of paper, then cut and glued to the model after you finish folding it.

Besides insignias or emblems, we can add details, such as a cabin or exhaust pipe. That is what we did for the Supermarine Spitfire.

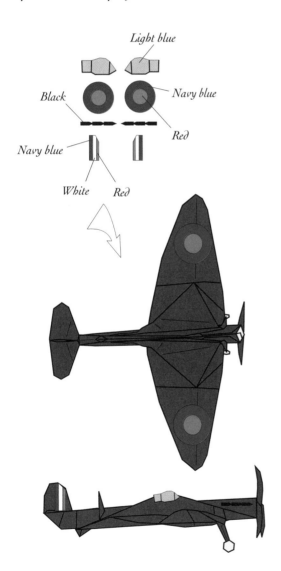

RAF insignias for the Spitfire

Another common technique involves getting the colors ready before folding the model. To do this, we must study the "crease pattern" of the figure and decide which side of the paper will be seen after it is folded. Here's an example of the prepared paper used to make a V-22 Osprey.

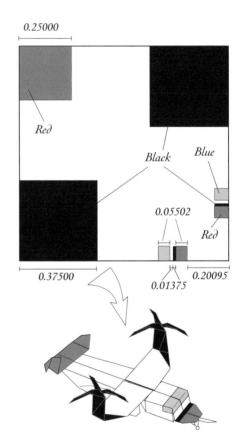

Color pattern for the V-22 Osprey

The two previous techniques can be combined. We did this in the Fokker Dr. 1. After preparing the paper, we get a brown propeller, shades of red for the wings, altitude rudder and fuselage, and a white guiding rudder. After folding the model, we can add Maltese crosses to the wings and to the tail.

Finally, we can varnish the model give it a more consistent appearance and to make it more resistant to the passage of time. We can apply airplane-modeling varnish with a brush or spray.

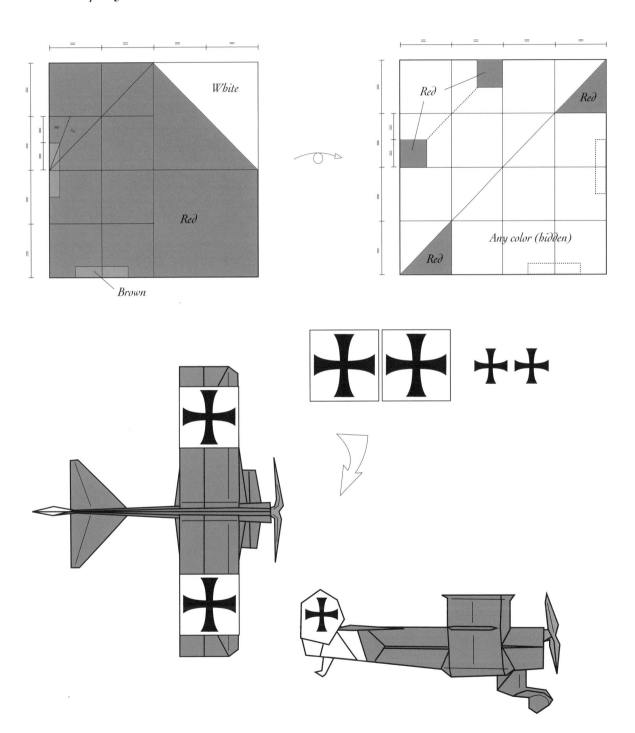

Fokker Dr. 1 color patterns and insignias

Photographs

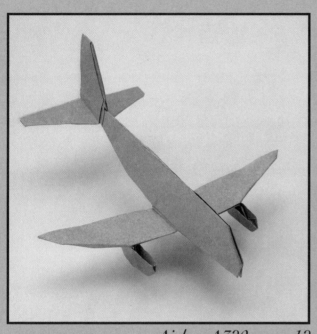

Airbus A320, page 12

F-117 Night Hawk, page 17

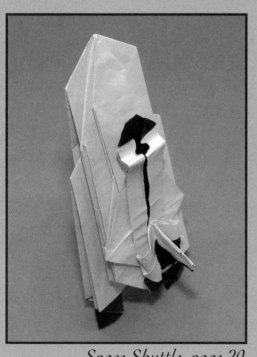

Space Shuttle, page 20

Bell Model 209 Huey Cobra, page 23

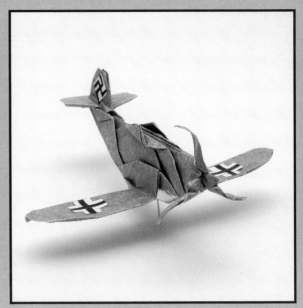

Messerschmitt Bf 109K, page 25

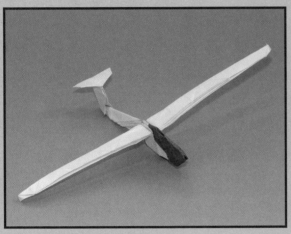

Engineless Glider, page 29

Supermarine Spitfire, page 32

Panavia Tornado, page 37

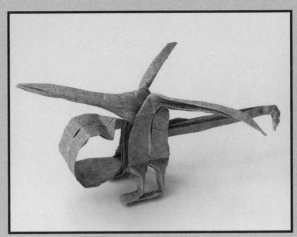

F-18 Hornet, page 42

Schweizer-Hughes 300, page 45

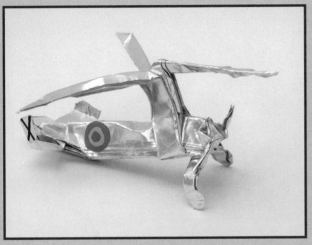

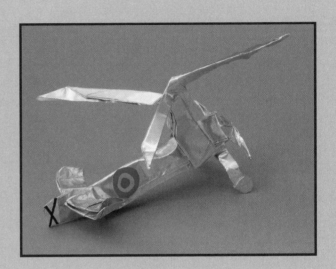

Autogyro Cierva C.30, page 48

Autogyro Cierva C.19, page 51

Eurofighter Typhoon, page 54

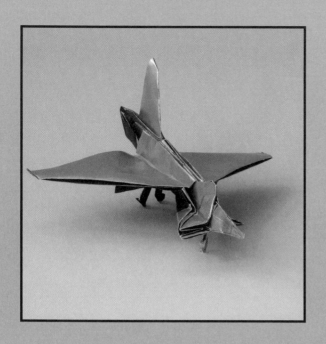

McDonnell Douglas MD-80, page 59

C-212 Aviocar, page 64

Bell/Boeing V-22 Osprey, Page 69

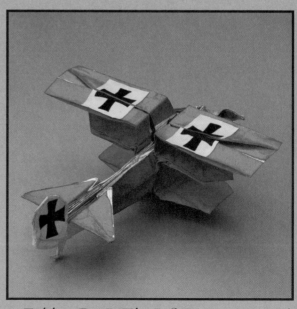

Fokker Dr. I, The Red Baron, page 74

Sopwith F.1 Camel,
page 79